WILLIAM BLAKE

William Vaughan

British Artists

Tate Gallery Publishing

For Rosie

Acknowledgements

My first debt is to my students, past and present, for the stimulating discussions that I have had with them about Blake over the years.

I am most grateful to Tate Publishing for including this book in their new British Artists series, and also to Richard Humphreys of the Tate Gallery, who arranged the commission and provided most helpful and illuminating comments on the first draft of the text. Robin Hamlyn has done a heroic job going through my text assiduously and saving me from many errors. I am also grateful to Sylvia Jaffrey for her careful and thoughtful copy-editing. Finally I would like to thank my editor, Liz Alsop, for having brought the book together and seen it through in such an exemplary manner.

William Vaughan

Front cover: *Pity* c.1795, detail (fig.32)

Back cover: *The Body of Abel Found by Adam and Eve* c.1826, detail (fig.3)

Frontispiece: John Linnell, *William Blake at Hampstead* c.1825, pencil 17.7 × 11.2 cm, Fitzwilliam Museum, Cambridge

Published by order of the Trustees of the Tate Gallery by

Tate Gallery Publishing Ltd
Millbank, London SW1P 4RG

© Tate Gallery. All rights reserved

The moral rights of the author have been asserted

ISBN 1 85437 281 5

A catalogue record for this book is available from the British Library

Cover design by Slatter-Anderson, London

Book design by James Shurmer

Printed in Hong Kong by South Seas International Press Ltd

Measurements are given in centimetres followed by inches in brackets, height before width

CONTENTS

INTRODUCTION

A New Kind of Artist

William Blake was a truly remarkable phenomenon. Equally gifted as poet and painter, he produced work as arresting for its beauty as for its strangeness. Even today, more than a century and a half after his death, he remains a controversial figure. For some he is an inspiring genius, a source of delight and insight. For others he is an unsettling eccentric, capable of some striking moments but also producing much that seems turgid and obscure. Blake can be many things, but supremely he is a challenge.

Blake was a visionary as well as an artist. That might not seem such an unusual thing to be. After all, do not all artists have their own peculiar kind of vision? Is it not the insight that we gain from their particular way of seeing that is of most value? This might be conventional wisdom nowadays, but not in Blake's time. At the end of the eighteenth century, when he was in his prime, artists were measured by different standards. They were judged by the norms of their practices. Poets were expected to write in recognised metres and to use traditional literary forms that could be classified by such terms as 'epic' or 'pastoral'. Painters were expected to conform to accepted standards of realistic representation, showing a knowledge of anatomy, perspective and time-honoured harmonious proportions. They were also meant to produce works that fell into categories or genres, that could be called 'landscape' or 'still life' or 'history' – the last of these illustrating well-known subjects from the past or from some famous author rather than depicting themes innovated by artists themselves.

Blake broke with these conventions in a way that no other painter or poet before him had done. He threw off what he called the 'bondage of Rhyming'[1] and the 'mathematic' forms of conventional visual art.[2] He invented his own subjects and transformed those that he took from others. Creativity and originality were all to him.

> I must Create a System, or be enslav'd by another Man's.
> I will not Reason & Compare: my business is to Create.[3]

He was a new kind of artist – a harbinger of what has since become a norm. Indeed, his example was one of the forces that helped to bring this change about. His art emphasises, time and again, the power of the imagination, that talisman for modern art. He encourages us to make a bold leap in our thinking to match that in his own. The story of his life – of a man living in poverty for his vision and persisting despite the near total neglect of his contemporaries – is an inspiring one that seems to encompass all that has come to be expected of the artist of integrity in recent times.

Inside the illustration, in script:

Enitharmon slept,
Eighteen hundred years: Man was a Dream!
The night of Nature and their harps unstrung:
She slept in middle of her nights song.
Eighteen hundred years, a female dream!

Shadows of men in fleeting bands upon the winds:
Divide the heavens of Europe:
Till Albions Angel smitten with his own plagues fled with his bands
The cloud bears hard on Albions shore:
Fill'd with immortal demons of futurity:
In council gather the smitten Angels of Albion
The cloud bears hard upon the council house; down rushing
On the heads of Albions Angels.

One hour they lay buried beneath the ruins of that hall:
But as the stars rise from the salt lake they arise in pain,
In troubled mists o'erclouded by the terrors of strugling times

1 *'Europe, a Prophecy':*
'Enitharmon Slept'
*c.*1821
Relief etching with
watercolour
30.4 × 23.6 (12 × 9¼)
Fitzwilliam Museum,
Cambridge

From many points of view we are in a better position to appreciate Blake than most of his contemporaries were. We can admire the power of his ideas without having to worry too much, perhaps, about whether they are true in a literal sense or not. We can be moved by the lyrical and rhythmic beauty in his verse without having to consider whether their metre is iambic or dactylic – or whether they scan at all. We can be exhilarated by the vibrant, flaming lines of what Blake called his 'Giant Forms' without having to be concerned about whether their musculature is correct or if the space they inhabit could really exist.

All this is gain. But it does not necessarily mean that he is understood any the better for it. Blake was an individualist who saw himself as out of step with his time. Yet in a fundamental way he was profoundly of his time. The very idea of the artist as an intransigent individualist emerged as a result of the intellectual and political ferment of his age. He lived in an age of revolutions; and if he expressed this revolution more fully in his practice than most artists did, he was only taking to an extreme things that others were also talking about and doing. Every stage of his career, every development that can be seen in his art, can be related to social, religious, political and artistic events that were going on in the world about him. And while he might have represented himself as an isolated, prophetic figure, he did not shut himself off from his times. He was deeply concerned about the major issues of his age and addressed them constantly in his art. It was, in his eyes, his spiritual duty to do so: 'Mark well my words – they are your eternal salvation', he advised in one of his prophetic books.[4] It was not his fault if others did not listen.

Blake's vision was utterly individual; but what he made and did was the outcome of his circumstances and experiences. He himself understood the importance of events and actions for making revelation possible. As he put it, 'Eternity is in love with the productions of time'.[5]

Of primary importance is the need to see Blake as a production of his own time, but not thereby to reduce him to a set of markers for charting artistic or socio-political developments. Blake was far too innovative and active to be diminished thus. He was radical in thought, word and deed. What he created came from his experiences and understanding. It did not, however, fit easily into any of the existing categories of production and expression available to him. This was not for want of trying. He made considerable

2 'Europe, a Prophecy':
Frontispiece,
'The Ancient of Days'
c.1821
Relief etching with
watercolour
30.4 × 23.6 (12 × 9¼)
Fitzwilliam Museum,
Cambridge

efforts – particularly in the earlier part of his life – to belong. Much of
the dynamism of his career comes from the dialogue between success and
failure that runs through it.

This book will follow the unfolding of that career, but it might be helpful
before embarking to consider one of the works of Blake's maturity to gain
an idea of the way his art functioned once it had developed.

The picture above – a hand-coloured relief etching – shows God creating
the world. He is seated in a circle – an ancient symbol for the
perfection of Heaven – and is stretching down from this with a pair of compasses into the darkness. This might seem to be a completely traditional
image. God the Father is often represented in medieval art measuring out
the earth with a pair of compasses, like an architect or master craftsman.

Another conventional feature of the work is the figure of God himself, which is modelled on the forms of Michelangelo, the great Renaissance artist Blake venerated above all others.

Despite this, the image is original in both its appearance and conception. It shows Blake's ability to see things anew, to read new meanings into old forms. Although the picture is popularly called *The Ancient of Days* this was not Blake's name for it. It actually represents Urizen, a figure invented by Blake himself to represent the harsh lawgiving deity who had produced the rule-bound world in which he found himself. This is not clear if the image is seen on its own; but it is when viewed in its original context. Blake designed it as a frontispiece to his book *Europe, a Prophecy* (1794), in which he describes how the baleful influence of Urizen had caused Europe to develop a repressive and materialistic society, 'smitten with plague' (see fig. 1). Eventually this had provoked the violent reaction of the French Revolution of 1789 – an event that had occurred five years previously and whose ramifications were far from resolved. Louis XVI had been executed in 1793, the Jacobin reign of terror was in full flood, and Europe had been plunged into war. Many former supporters of revolution and reform had scuttled to conservatism in the face of such occurrences. Blake, however, who remained true to his radical ideals, saw things differently. He looked beyond the event to its causes, perceiving repressive authority to be at the heart of the catastrophe. He mythologised events, but did not obscure or confuse what he was talking about.

Even without a knowledge of Blake's *Europe* and the context of this image, we can still be impressed by its awesome splendour. The powerful design, in which God's arm presses down the divider with the force of a piston, has all the 'fearful symmetry' that Blake had recently ascribed to the 'Tyger' in his famous poem about that animal (fig. 23). In a masterful touch he has made God's beard and hair stream to the left as if caught up in a gigantic wind. Once the Deity leans out of his sanctum in eternity, it seems, he too can be buffeted by time. Clouds of dark foreboding surround the heavenly circle and all but obscure its light. None of its luminescence reaches down to the area of blackness in which the harsh lawgiver is measuring out his soul-destroying world of regulation. Finally the colours used reinforce the picture's sombre meaning. Oppressive blacks and reds predominate, while the golden tones of Heaven look sickly and weak against them.

Images such as this confirm that Blake's art has real pictorial power. This is not a case of some mystic who happened also to scrawl out patterns and scribble down fantastic predictions. Blake brought a true artistic imagination and a thorough professionalism to his creations. His skills grew slowly and progressively, and it is the changing stages of this development that provide the most useful framework against which to view his art.

1
LEARNING

Origins

William Blake was born in Soho, in the centre of London, on 28 November 1757. He died in the same city nearly seventy years later, on 12 August 1827. His origins were humble – his father was a hosier – and he remained poor all his life. Trained as an engraver, he practised this craft until his dying day, working mostly on a freelance basis, making reproductions, and copying the designs of others for tradesmen, publishers and printsellers. 'The engraver Blake' is how he was described habitually in his lifetime. The facets of his output that we value most today – the original prints and paintings, the prophecies and poetry – were produced in addition to this and accounted for very little of his income. Such magnificent works as *The Body of Abel Found by Adam and Eve* (fig. 3) were regarded as eccentricities by most people who encountered them.

The vast discrepancy between his inner and outer worlds is encountered in all aspects of his life. He rarely left London. The only extended time that he was away was between 1800 and 1803 when he attempted to settle in the country. Yet in his mind he ranged as freely as any, building a cosmology that reached beyond space and time. Closer to home, he was keenly aware of and involved in the great social and political upheavals of his age. A political freethinker, he supported the French Revolution on its outbreak in 1789 and remained a radical sympathiser throughout the dark times that followed. He saw London develop from a lively commercial community to an alienating modern metropolis and censured in his poems the evils that arose in the wake of this transformation in his poems. Living through the early stages of the Industrial Revolution he witnessed the beginnings of the soul-destroying effects of mechanisation. It was this, perhaps, more than anything else that convinced him that the artist had a new role in the modern world, one in which he or she would become the guardian of the spirit and the imagination.

Much of Blake's perception can be related to his personal circumstances and background. The craftsman community from which he came was one of those most likely to support political radicalism at the time. Highly skilled and industrious, its members saw themselves particularly at risk in the emerging capitalist economy. They welcomed the ideas of those who promoted a new kind of social order that would reverse the growing class distinctions. Blake also absorbed his strong sense of religion from his background. The craftsman community was a devout one, largely inspired by the enthusiasm and egalitarianism of nonconformist sects. It would seem that Blake's family had a connection with the Muggletonians, a radical

religious group that had emerged during the period of revolution in Britain in the seventeenth century. In any case, they were clearly dissenters. This background also affected Blake's idea of poetry. From early on he had a thorough knowledge of the King James Bible of 1611 and 1612. That literary masterpiece gave him his first experience of the spiritual poetically expressed.

The seeds of Blake's radicalism, religious ardour and tireless industry were undoubtedly sown in his childhood. But from the start there were also ways in which he was different from his family and friends. He was a sensitive child and showed artistic talent from an early age, so much so that at the age of 10 he was sent by his parents to Henry Pars's drawing school in the Strand. But what singled him out most of all was his tendency to have visions. Perhaps not surprisingly this was viewed with alarm by his father, who gave his 10-year-old son a sound thrashing when told that he had seen angels in a tree on Peckham Rye. Such treatment can only have helped to strengthen Blake's growing opposition to authoritarianism wherever he encountered it.

Blake's claim to see visions remains contentious. Was he simply making them up (as his father clearly believed), or were they genuine experiences? In his recent biography of Blake,[1] Peter Ackroyd points out that what psychologists call eidetic vision – the ability to project mental images so that they appear to be part of the external world – is a condition

4 *The Ghost of
a Flea c.*1819
Tempera and gold
on panel
21.4 × 16.2
$(8\frac{3}{8} \times 6\frac{1}{2})$
Tate Gallery

encountered fairly frequently in childhood. What was unusual in Blake was that he retained this capability in adulthood and late in life he drew pictures of his visions for his friend, the astrologer John Varley (see fig.4).

We cannot determine the degree or manner in which Blake experienced his visions. On some occasions in later life he seems to have been making up, or at least enhancing, what he claimed to see. On occasions, too, he appeared to accept that his experiences were largely the products of his imagination – and this probably helped him to elide the line between self-willed envisionings and involuntary experiences. Yet, whatever they were, these visions did help him centre his art on the mystic experience. Vision, for Blake, was an essential part of creativity. It brought into being that which could not be produced by reason alone. Like the prophets of the Old Testament he was a seer who could penetrate the everyday to perceive mysteries beyond. In one of his aphorisms, Blake emphasised the division between what could be achieved by mere thought and cleverness – which he characterised as talent – and that which could be achieved by the perceptions of genius: 'Talent thinks, genius sees'.[2]

Blake's emphasis on vision was to some extent a product of his time. The instability that followed the French Revolution – as well as the co-incidental approach of the year 1800 – sparked off a wave of popular millennialism, the belief that the Second Coming was nigh. A number of millennialist prophets came to the fore at this time, notably Richard Brothers and Joanna Southcott. Yet Blake differed from such people in his emphasis on the inner world. His revolution was essentially one of the mind. He combined the traditions of mystical radicalism – which can be traced back in Western society to the Middle Ages and are probably a phenomenon in all communities – with the concept of artistic creativity. This again can be seen as a product of his unique position, for as well as coming from a radical and religious craftsman background – and probably genuinely experiencing the effects of eidetic vision in childhood – he had absorbed new ideas about artistic genius from the more educated milieu he encountered in early manhood. That great cultural movement that – for better or worse – is usually characterised by the term 'Romanticism' pioneered a new perception of the innate, and of the notion of creative genius as a quality quite separate from rational process. As will be seen, Blake knew of such original and rebellious artists as John Mortimer, James Barry and Henry Fuseli when he was forming his ideas. However, while these others subscribed to the idea of creative originality, none linked

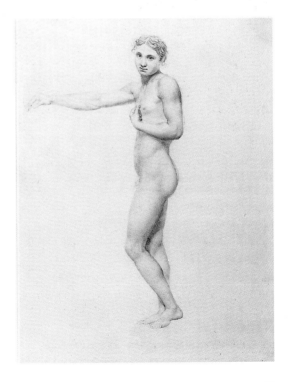

5 *Academy Study:*
A Naked Youth Seen
from the Side, perhaps
Robert Blake
*c.*1779–80
Black chalk
47.9 × 37
(18⅞ × 14¼)
British Museum

artistic genius to prophecy in the same manner as Blake; but then none lived half-way between the worlds of popular millennialism and high culture in the way that Blake increasingly did.

Blake's unusual position left him peculiarly isolated – something that might well have destroyed a person with fewer inner resources. Nowadays, when he is an acknowledged master of English art and literature, it is common to talk of Blake's 'circle', as though he was in his lifetime the hub of some creative movement. In reality he was on the periphery of a large number of different groups and tolerated on the whole only as a marginal figure. Blake had many acquaintances, but few, if any, intimate friends. The two people closest to him were both members of his family and in subordinate positions to him. One was his brother Robert, ten years his junior and possibly the model of one of his life-drawings (fig. 5), who died in 1787 at the age of 20. The other was his wife, Catherine Boucher, a gentle and unchallenging presence. The daughter of a market gardener, she had few pretensions but shared Blake's enthusiasm for the spiritual. She was, in the traditional sense, his helpmate, who learned to assist him in the production of his work and seems to have endured poverty with rare fortitude. However, she was hardly in a position to debate or dispute his ideas. Intellectually, Blake was on his own.

6 *Joseph of Arimathea among the Rocks of Albion*
*c.*1773
Engraving
25.9 × 14.2
(10¼ × 5⅝)
Fitzwilliam Museum, Cambridge

Training

'Man brings All he has and can have Into the World with him', Blake wrote in fury in the margin of his copy of Sir Joshua Reynolds's *Discourses on Art*.[3] But that was in middle life, when he had perhaps forgotten how much he had had to learn in his youth.

That Blake should have been apprenticed to an engraver was in itself a telling choice. Engraving was a lowlier craft than painting, and one that more frequently attracted youths from Blake's background. Apprenticeship was cheaper, and there was more chance of steady employment afterwards. There is a story that Blake himself elected to become apprenticed to an engraver rather than a painter because he was aware his father could not really afford the cost of the latter. Whether this is true or not, it certainly seems clear that he always had the ambition to be an original and inventive artist, and never expected engraving to limit him to the mere reproduction of other people's work.

Blake was apprenticed to James Basire in 1772, when he was 15, and served his time for seven years. Basire was a rather old-fashioned engraver who gave Blake a sound and thorough knowledge of line engraving on copper. Blake's detractors often see those paintings and prints made by methods of his own invention as naive and even rather amateurish in execution; but no one could deny the professionalism and technical mastery of his conventional work on copper. In the publishing world he had a reputation for clarity and exactness – even if some found his sense of form and insistent detail somewhat unnerving.

Blake's mastery of copper-engraving seems to have provided the basis for one of the most characteristic and admirable features of his pictorial style – his sinuous flowing line. Copper-engraving consists largely of gouging grooves with a graver in the soft metal. As the graver moves along, its direction is to some extent guided by the groove that has already been cut. This makes it easier to execute regular or slowly changing curves than to effect abrupt shifts in direction. For the latter to be achieved it is necessary to lift the graver out of the groove and start again. This encourages a more regulated form of line-production than is common in such printmaking techniques as etching or lithography, or in drawings made with pen or pencil. Anyone looking at a Blake copper-engraving will be impressed by the power of these sinuous lines and the splendid tonal webs they can create together, like voices singing in contrapuntal harmony.

Blake's experience as an engraver also affected his attitude to copying. He spent most of his professional career reproducing the drawings and paintings of others. Given his views on vision and originality, this might seem to have been a humiliating enslavement. But Blake, characteristically, saw the matter differently, and made a virtue of necessity. Copying for him was not a mindless bondage. It was reinterpreting, seeing anew. It was as though, by copying an image intensely, you could see right through it to something beyond. While an apprentice he produced as a technical exercise a copy of an engraving based on a figure by Michelangelo from the Pauline Chapel in the Vatican (fig.6). Blake reproduced the form meticulously, but the figure ceased to be that intended by Michelangelo and became instead a figure on a seashore, later identified as Joseph of Arimathea landing on the shores of Albion. It is at the same time a meticulous copy and an original invention.

Blake's originality, in fact, did not involve a rejection of the past, but rather a re-engagement with it. He made copies for pleasure and personal enlightenment as well as a professional duty. Despite his poverty, he was a connoisseur of drawings and prints, making purchases in shops and salerooms from early adolescence onwards. He built up a remarkable collection which, sadly, had to be sold in the last years of his life when he was almost completely out of funds. Some of his acquisitions were works by acknowledged masters – such as Michelangelo himself. Others were of less well-known artists, such as the great northern Renaissance printmakers Albrecht Dürer and Lucas van Leyden. He was ahead of his time in recognising their merits.

Blake's apprenticeship also brought him into contact with an art form then out of fashion – the Gothic style of the Middle Ages. James Basire was at the time executing a series of engravings for the Society of Antiquaries recording the medieval royal tombs in Westminster Abbey. Blake was detailed to make drawings from these in preparation for the engravings. That Blake was sent to do such work suggests that he must have been well regarded by his master, and must have been seen as one of the most accomplished draughtsmen in his workshop. It is hard to determine exactly which drawings Blake made, but some seem to show what was to become his unmistakable line, such as that of *Countess Aveline* (fig.7). Blake later adapted the elegant, elongated curves of such works to suggest figures inflamed by the spiritual.

Blake's appreciation of Gothic art grew with time. Near the end of his life he coined the aphorism 'Grecian is Mathematic Form: Gothic is Living Form'.[4] By this time Gothic had come to occupy a place in his mythology as an ideal of spiritual and living art to be contrasted with what he then saw as the dull and mechanical art of the materialistic classical world. This view of Gothic as the art of an age of faith was common amongst medieval revivalists after 1800. But when Blake was an apprentice in the 1770s such a movement was only in its infancy. There is no sign, either, that Blake had turned against the classical world at that time. It would be truer to say that he saw both Greek and Gothic as great inspirational art at the beginning of his career.

Blake's feeling for gothic sinuousness was probably a hindrance – maybe even a fatal one – in his next career move. After he had completed his apprenticeship as an engraver in 1779, he enrolled as a student at the Royal Academy of Art. This could be seen as an attempt to shift practices. Having trained as a craftsman, he now wished to initiate his career as a fine artist. The Academy was still relatively young at that time – it had been founded eleven years previously in 1768 – but it was already having an immense impact on artistic life in Britain. For the first time there was a proper professional organisation for artists. Membership was an honour – limited to forty leading members of the profession. But as well as this it organised an annual exhibition in which 'the best' art was shown, and it ran a school for educating young artists along the lines laid down during the Renaissance. For generations British artists had cried out for the kind

7 *Countess Aveline, Effigy in Westminster Abbey seen from Above* 1775
Pen and sepia wash
25.7 × 7.8
($10\frac{1}{8} \times 3\frac{1}{8}$)
Society of Antiquaries of London

of status and training that their colleagues in Italy and France had enjoyed for centuries. Now at last it seemed as though their call had been answered.

The Aspirant History Painter

Blake must have enrolled at the Academy with high hopes, as did so many other young artists of his generation. Like most of these, he was to be bitterly disappointed; for the Academy did not deliver what it promised. Worse than this, it seemed in the eyes of its critics to be preventing precisely the developments that it had been set up to encourage. The president, Sir Joshua Reynolds, praised historical painting loudly. It was, he said, the noblest activity for an artist and young aspirants should live on bread and water, if necessary, in order to pursue so noble a calling. Yet he himself dwelt in luxury on the proceeds of his practice as a fashionable portrait painter. The truth of the matter was that there were few opportunities for a history painter in eighteenth-century Britain. In France and many other European countries this difficult and exacting profession was supported largely by official patronage – either that of the ruler or the church. But in Britain the constitutional monarchy did not have the power to order vast and expensive decorations of royal palaces in the way that Louis XIV and his successors had done in France. Furthermore, the established Anglican church was sufficiently Protestant in inclination to take a dim view of using art for devotional purposes. By encouraging young British artists to specialise the Royal Academy was preparing them for a practice for which there was virtually no outlet. It was also preparing them badly for the task; for the training offered there was no more than a pale imitation of the more rigorous system that the academies of continental Europe usually offered their students. The main outcome of the system set up by the Academy was the production of generations of poorly trained, unemployable historical artists. Most gave up the struggle and turned to more profitable work. But a few determined souls persisted in poverty and misery.

Most of this sad story lay in the future. At the time Blake was a student it still seemed as though history painting could offer a bright career for young hopefuls. There was a generation of painters about fifteen to twenty years ahead of him who had already thrown themselves into imaginative historical work and seemed to be showing what could be done. The most successful was Benjamin West (1738–1820), the American painter who had achieved an international success with his innovative modern history painting *The Death of General Wolfe* when it was exhibited in 1771[5] and had subsequently become historical painter to George III, in a private capacity. West had studied in Rome and when not painting modern history (which in fact he rarely did), he often produced pictures in a severe classical mode that was much emulated. Blake was among the emulators on occasion – but he was more drawn to other, slightly younger historical aspirants. The brilliant and eccentric John Hamilton Mortimer (1740–79), who died young in the year Blake enrolled at the Academy, had painted dramatic

8 After John Hamilton Mortimer (1740–79) by Joseph Haynes, *Death on a Pale Horse* 1784 Etching 70.5 × 50.8 (27¼ × 20), British Museum

Death on a Pale Horse

9 Henry Fuseli (1741–1825) *The Nightmare* (second version) 1791 Oil on canvas 75.5 × 64 (29¾ × 25¼) Frankfurter Goethe Museum

scenes. Perhaps more importantly he had issued a series of etchings of heads of figures from Shakespeare (1775–6). His *Death on a Pale Horse* (fig.8) – based on the figure from the *Apocalypse* – became a classic image of sublime horror.[6] Amongst the living, there were other figures who were equally inspiring. The Swiss painter Johann Heinrich Füßli (or Henry Fuseli, as he styled himself in Britain) (1741–1825) had recently returned from study at Rome. A man of formidable intellect and learning, he specialised in sensational and dramatic works, sometimes on subjects of his own invention. In 1782, when Blake was a student at the Academy, Fuseli exhibited there the work that was to gain him international renown, *The Nightmare* (fig.9). Later in life the two were to have a complex personal and artistic interrelationship. At this point, when Blake was an obscure young student, the older artist must have been an inspiring example of what could be done. A third influence was the Irish artist James Barry (1741–1806). Like Fuseli and West, Barry had studied in Rome and was full of the classical ideal. In 1782 he became Professor of Painting at the Academy – a hopeful sign that the institution was now taking rigorous historical painting seriously. Even more exciting was Barry's decision to defy the patronage system and go it alone. Unable to find official support to paint a vast mural, he had offered to do one free of charge on the walls of the Society of Arts (see fig.10). Unlike Reynolds, Barry was prepared to starve for his principles. The venture bankrupted him. Surviving to this day in the now Royal Society of Arts, this vast scheme is still an underrated work. Executed in a rigorous classical style, it shows the 'Progress of Human

Knowledge' from Ancient Greece to modern-day Britain. Heroic both in scale and ambition, it demonstrated that a British artist could handle the Grand Manner in the way that the old masters had done.

Sadly for Barry, this cycle did not lead to a flood of commissions for similar work. He remained without serious employment. In later life he became increasingly bitter about Reynolds and the Royal Academy. A confirmed republican, he resented the Academy's linking of the profession with royal patronage as well as the duplicity of an organisation that ostensibly supported high art but in practice pandered more to power and fashion. Whereas the Academy was set up with the intention of promoting the public position of art, it functioned more like an exclusive gentleman's

10 James Barry
(1741–1806)
*Crowning of the Victors
at Olympia* (detail
including self-portrait)
1777–84
Oil mural
Royal Society for the
encouragement of Arts,
Manufactures and
Commerce

11 *The Penance
of Jane Shore in
St Paul's Church*
c.1793
Watercolour and ink
(varnished)
24.5 × 29.5
(9⅝ × 11⅝)
Tate Gallery

12 *Oberon, Titania and Puck with Fairies Dancing c.*1785–90
Pencil and water-colour
47.5 × 67.5
(18¼ × 26⅝)
Tate Gallery

club. Barry became increasingly critical of the institution in his lectures to the students and in the end steps were taken to silence him. He has the rare distinction of being the only artist in the whole history of the Academy to have been expelled from its ranks. By then he was an old and broken man.

Blake was a constant admirer of Barry and lamented the fate that befell him. Around 1780, when Barry was at the height of his powers he must have been a charismatic example for young aspirants. Blake, now 23, aimed to be a historical artist like Barry and paint huge epic cycles similar to those going up on the walls of the Society of Arts. He began to plan a cycle of illustrations to the history of England, and mapped out his designs in watercolour. *The Penance of Jane Shore* (fig.11) is one of these. Like so many images in the series, it dwells upon a person oppressed by authority and convention. Jane Shore was the mistress of Edward IV who was arrested by the future Richard III in 1483 and publicly humiliated. Blake shows her walking through the streets of London holding a candle and wrapped in a white sheet as part of her penance. His source for this subject – as for most of the cycle – was Rapin de Thoyras's popular *History of England*. In this it is stated that Jane Shore 'behaved with such modesty and decency, that such as respected her Beauty more than her fault, never were in greater admiration of her, than now'.[7] Blake suggests sympathy for her through the expressions of both the soldiers who accompany her and the crowd that watches. Doubtless he was using this image as part of his protest against orthodox sexual morality. He was already moving in radical political circles at this time.

The original design for this work is known now only in a sketch. But the Tate Gallery has a worked-up version, probably executed later, in 1793. Its flat, frieze-like design shows the extent to which Blake was following at that time the fashionable classical style. This was held to be the purest and most

elevated for historical art. Based on the friezes of Ancient Greece, it reduced the visual to a primitive clarity and purity. One of his close friends at this time was the sculptor John Flaxman (1755–1826). A fellow student at the Royal Academy, Flaxman went to Rome in 1787 where he developed further a pure classical style. Soon afterwards he was to achieve international fame when, in 1793, engravings were published after the *Outlines* that he had designed illustrating scenes from Homer and Dante (see fig.16). Throughout the early 1780s Blake continued to design scenes from British history, Shakespeare (see fig.12) and the Bible using the simplified classical style. These culminated in the three watercolour illustrations to the biblical story of Joseph (see fig.13) which were exhibited at the Academy in 1785. These works represent his most serious attempt to gain acceptance as a historical artist. They are highly wrought, and have the strict, frieze-like design then expected of progressive historical painting. It is worth remembering that they were being painted at the same time as Jacques-Louis David in France was completing and exhibiting his celebrated *Oath of the Horatii*, 1784, the work that sealed his success as the leading Neoclassical historical artist in France. David – who had all the advantages of the French system of public patronage behind him – was executing a huge canvas commissioned in the name of the Monarchy. But in concept the two are not so far apart. They use figures viewed side-on to tell a dramatic moment in the story. In the case of Blake it is the moment when Joseph

21

reveals his identity to his brothers and forgives them for their transgressions against him. Joseph – who was sold into slavery by his jealous brothers but eventually triumphed over them – might have attracted Blake as a person who was rejected but overcame adversity and then forgave his oppressors. Perhaps by this time he was already sensing oppression. Certainly the reception of these works did little to assuage such a feeling. Apparently Sir Joshua Reynolds himself expressed disapproval. It was the end of his hopes as a history painter.

Since Blake's style at this time can be associated with the fashionable classical taste of the time – and bears evident affinities with work by both Barry and Flaxman – it might be asked why his pictures were so poorly received. The most likely answer is that even at this stage his handling of human anatomy appeared (to put it politely) deviant. For while he had imitated the simple arrangement of Classical art, his figures lack the strict anatomical exactness then expected of proper historical art. The taste for the gothic flowing line seems constantly to be taking over, giving a charm and expressive power to the designs but appearing to the likes of Reynolds to smack of incompetence. Flaxman's designs, for all their simplicity, never exhibit similar deviancies. They are always 'correct' in their anatomy and sense of classical proportion – something that nowadays seems to limit their expressive power.

One incident must have made it clear to Blake more than any other how isolated he had become. Throughout the 1780s British artists were becoming increasingly excited by a new possibility for the financing of history painting. This was not some major publicly funded scheme; everyone knew that was impossible. Rather it was a commercial enterprise dreamed up by the engraver and city alderman John Boydell. Boydell had made a fortune through his print business and sensed that history painting could be supported by the market, through the sale of engraved copies after pictures. This was, in effect, the kind of breakthrough that had been pioneered by Hogarth a generation earlier with the sale of prints after his 'Modern Moral Subjects' such as the *Harlot's Progress*. It was Boydell's idea to capitalise on the interest that had been aroused in serious history painting by the Academy and Reynolds's rhetoric on the one hand and in the revived interest in Shakespeare on the other. He commissioned leading historical artists of the day to depict scenes from Shakespeare. These were engraved and sold in book form. The paintings them-selves were exhibited in a special gallery as a permanent exhibition. It was a bold venture. There were critics, of

14 James Gillray (1756–1815) *Shakespeare-Sacrificed; or The Offering to Avarice* 1789 Etching 47.3 × 37.5 ($18\frac{5}{8}$ × $14\frac{3}{4}$) British Museum

SHAKESPEARE - SACRIFICED; - or - The Offering to AVARICE.

course. The satirist James Gillray depicted Boydell sacrificing Shakespeare on the altar of avarice (fig.14). But it was at least a way of making history painting visible. For a time the prints sold well. However, Boydell never did manage to recoup his outlay – largely due to a decline in sales to continental Europe caused by the Napoleonic Wars – and in the end the paintings had to be auctioned off.

Boydell employed a very wide range of artists, including established figures such as Fuseli, West, Reynolds and Barry, together with young hopefuls such as James Northcote and Richard Westall. Blake's name is conspicuously absent from the list. Worse than this, he was not even one of those employed to make an engraving after the designs of the others. It was clear from these omissions that Blake had been passed over, both as artist and engraver, as someone suitable for historical work.

Surviving Failure

By the time that he was 30, in 1787, Blake had suffered three major setbacks to his professional ambitions as well as a deep personal loss. But, as Noel Coward once put it, 'a successful man is one who survives his failures'.

The first major setback was the one already discussed; the failure to make a mark as a history painter. The second was the failure to establish a business as an engraver. Blake originally set up with James Parker, a fellow apprentice, in 1784, but at some point in the following years the partnership was dissolved. This collapse was more significant than it might seem at first. There was great wealth to be made in those days from a flourishing engraving business – as could be seen from the career of Alderman Boydell. On the other hand, a mere jobbing engraver without any personal resources would be exploited and would make very little money indeed. The engraving business was as ruthless as any other in those days of mounting capitalism and the engraver who was a worker rather than a master could expect little more than a life of grind and misery. This was the world Blake fell into by failing to establish himself as the master of his own business.

The third setback was in poetry. Already, while still an apprentice, Blake had attracted attention with his gift for lyrical verse. In the early 1780s he was taken up by certain liberal intellectuals of the day. He could be found at the salon of Mrs Mathew, a celebrated bluestocking. Interest in him grew to the extent that funds were found to publish a volume of his works – *Poetical Sketches*. Although these were printed – with the date of 1783 – it seems they were never properly published. Somehow interest in Blake the poet had drifted away.

It is hard to determine quite why this was the case, but it would seem that in the end he turned out to be too alarming a phenomenon to fit easily into the pattern of patronage that had been mapped out for him. Amongst liberal and progressive intellectual circles, there was a great vogue for 'noble savages'. The idea of the Swiss-French philosopher Jean-Jacques Rousseau, that man was fundamentally good and had been corrupted by society, was supported by the discovery of native poetic talents who could then be lionised for a time and made into society darlings. There are many peasant and artisan poets of the eighteenth century – such as the ploughboy Stephen Duck and the shoemaker Richard Bloomfield – who fitted this image. Unlearned, they were taken up, trained and educated, expressed their gratitude and then often settled down to comfortable careers. There were other peasant poets who were originally patronised in this way but who proved too unruly to contain, such as Robert Burns and John Clare. Blake belonged with the latter. By all accounts his strangeness began to upset and tire people in Mrs Mathew's circle and support drifted away. Apart from any loss in terms of poetic success, there is another that occurred as a result of this collapse. According to contemporary accounts, Blake would sometimes sing his poems to tunes of his own invention. None of these survive. Blake himself could not write music down, and clearly no one with the appropriate skills considered the eccentric's melodies worth recording.

These setbacks would have broken many people, but Blake managed to turn them into a strength. Indeed, in retrospect, we may be grateful that he did not experience conventional success in any of these fields, since if he had done so he might never have gone on to create those achievements for which he is now known. Had he become successful as a history painter he might have turned into another Mortimer, Fuseli or Barry, producing historical pieces that would now be of interest only to the specialist. Had he succeeded at running a printing business he might have ended up a wealthy and overworked manager, supervising the work of others – as Boydell did – and perhaps regretting occasionally that he no longer had the time to play at penning poems and drafting designs as he had done in his careless youth. Had he succeeded as a peasant poet he might indeed have become another Duck or Bloomfield, producing harmless, charming lyrics for the delight of the more enlightened of the professional classes. None of these Blakes would have held a candle to the one we have today.

Blake certainly must have suffered immensely from these setbacks. But they were thrown into a more manageable perspective by both the joys and sadnesses of his personal life. In 1782 he had the joy of getting married. As has already been mentioned, his wife Catherine was a constant source of support to him. Sadness was brought by the death, in 1787, of his brother Robert. Ten years younger than Blake himself, Robert was almost as much Blake's son as brother. He had educated him, trained him in his craft and had hoped to have him work as a companion. When Robert died Blake was profoundly moved. More than that, he began to have visions of his dead brother. This may indeed be the real moment at which he became a serious visionary. Like many who lose a loved one, part of Blake died with Robert. That part went – in conformity with his beliefs – to the other world. From that time onwards Blake believed he had a direct line to eternity. As is typical of such situations, he claimed his brother Robert appeared to him in dreams, and in one instance showed him the unique printing method he devised for his original work.

2
REVOLUTION

Vision and Independence

'Joys impregnate. Sorrows bring forth.'[1] In sorrow and loss Blake began to bring forth. He survived his failures not by turning his back on what he had done before, but by reworking experiences and using them again in new and far more powerful ways. The separate fragments of history painting, engraving and poetry now came together to form a totality of his own fashioning. Gradually he realised he had everything to hand to practise on his own, to forge images and verse and present these to the public directly through his professional expertise as a printmaker.

He was, however, a line engraver and not a typographer, and this is probably why he devised a method of his own for making prints that combined picture and text. Unlike conventional copperplate printing, his method involved writing or drawing on the copper with stopping-out solution, a special acid-resistant ink. Then the plate would be put in an acid bath, where those sections that had not been written or drawn upon would be eaten away, leaving the rest standing up in relief. These were the parts that would then be printed from, using the surface printing method normal for letterpress. Blake had a small printing press and could perform this task in his own home. Subsequently the designs would be hand-coloured either by Blake or by his wife.

The technique was a tricky one, and at first the results – a group of prose tracts of which possibly the first were the booklets *There is No Natural Religion* and *All Religions are One* – were quite crude. In time he improved his mastery of the method greatly. However, the plates must always have had an amateurish look about them when compared to the high-quality professional printing of the period.

This particular form of self-publication was unique. Yet the idea of printing and distributing one's own work was not as unusual then as it is now. Small-scale printing and publishing was common, and booksellers and printshops habitually published their own work. The 1780s were a time of expanding published commentary on public events. Even before the outbreak of the French Revolution in 1789 there were major political upheavals that stimulated such output. America had won independence from Britain. The Gordon Riots had spread terror throughout London. The King had gone mad. Organised parliamentary opposition was growing. On all sides, it would seem, authority was being challenged and showing instability. Blake knew the world of protest well, as he moved in the circle of the radical publisher Joseph Johnson. This was the circle that contained such radical freethinkers as Tom Paine, supporter of revolution and author of *Rights of Man* (1791), and Mary Wollstonecraft, the campaigner for women's rights. Much of Blake's satirical work comes close to this world of political polemics.

The climate of dissent was a leading factor in the emergence of a vigorous form of pictorial political satire, particularly in the cartoons of James Gillray (see fig.14). Gillray, who was much the same age as Blake and had, like him, briefly been a student at the Royal Academy, was in his way providing a visionary alternative to the establishment in his fantastic images of political leaders which had certain affinities with the more satirical side of Blake. Yet Gillray – who played to a fashionable audience – had a wide circulation for his prints, while Blake had almost none.

Painting and Poetry; The Sister Arts

Blake's publications also differed from those of the other satirists and pamphleteers in the way that he combined word and image, using the latter to surround and elaborate the text of the former. The association between painting and poetry is a traditional one that can be traced back to antiquity where it received its classic formulation in the phrase of the Roman poet Horace, *Ut poesis pictura*, an invocation to poets to study the forms of the visual arts in order to mimic their command of overall effect. In the later eighteenth century the notion had been revived vigorously.

15 *The Resurrection of the Dead; Alternative Design for the title-page to Blair's 'The Grave',* 1806
Watercolour
42.5 × 31
(16¾ × 12¼)
British Museum

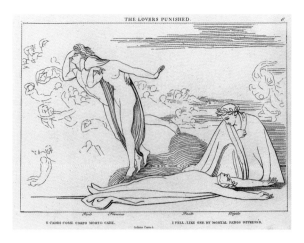

16 After John
Flaxman
(1755–1826)
by Thomas Piroli,
*Compositions from
the Hell, Purgatory,
and Paradise of Dante
Alighieri: Paolo and
Francesca Leaving
Dante (Inferno
Canto 5, line 142)*
1793
Engraving
29.2 × 45.5
(11½ × 17⅞)
British Museum

It had a particular attraction amongst visual artists as a means of enhancing their status. Reversing the original meaning of the phrase, they used it to assert that they were, in effect, pictorial poets. Sir Joshua Reynolds in his discourses had reclassified history painting as a form of poetry, and painters of grand historical cycles, such as Barry, liked to see themselves as creating the equivalent of an epic. The ramifications within the visual arts were profound. One can even claim that landscape painting rose to the heights that it did in the early nineteenth century because its practitioners could see themselves as producing a pictorial equivalent to the nature poetry that then formed such a strong part of British cultural life. On a commercial level, there was also a decided advantage in the pairing of the arts since it gave a context for producing elaborate and popular visual productions of poems – such as those Blake himself made for Blair's *The Grave* (fig.15) which actually made poetry more saleable. Rendering poetry in visual form could be seen as a kind of translation. This undoubtedly strengthened the hand of Boydell in producing his Shakespeare and of Flaxman in drawing his *Outlines* to Homer and Dante (see fig.16).

Blake's combination of word and image in his self-produced books was not therefore out of line either with the ambitions of fine artists generally at that time or with commercial practice. However, what is unusual is the extent to which he took the association. Many sources have been claimed for Blake's peculiarly intimate combination of image and text here. Medieval illuminated manuscripts must surely be the most powerful of these. It is unclear what precisely he might have known of such work. However, Blake was a constant visitor to sales and printshops, and could certainly have seen examples at the shop of one of his later employers, the publisher Richard Edwards who commissioned Blake to make border illustrations for Young's *Night Thoughts* (see fig.17). The elaborate intertwining of text and decoration in baroque title pages has also been cited as an influence. But whatever sources inspired Blake, he used them to develop something quite his own. His own position as being equally gifted in both enabled him to explore the interchange in a unique manner.

For with him painting was not simply the illustration of poetry, or even its rival. It was a counterpart, a genuine other half. Indeed, one might see the relationship as that of two voices singing a duet. At one point the two will sing in unison. At other points a harmony will be set up between the two. Sometimes one performs a counterpoint against the tune of the other. Sometimes a tune begun by one will be completed by the other.

These associations can be seen perhaps at their most integrated in the *Songs of Innocence and of Experience.* This collection of short lyrical verses is the most accessible of all Blake's works and has always been his most popular production. It began life as two separate works. The first, *Songs of Innocence*, was produced in 1789. It is in the pastoral mode. The narrator is a shepherd who receives inspiration from a child in a cloud to pipe his songs celebrating the divine in all creation (see fig.18). The book is small and narrow, with short-lined lyrics and illustrations. This format, together with the idyllic tone of the poetry and the title itself might lead one to suppose that it was intended to be a book for children. Blake was familiar with the genre, having produced illustrations for a child's book of similar shape and appearance by Mary Wollstonecraft, *Original Stories from Real Life*, a progressive tract promoting liberal education (see fig.19). Perhaps Blake set out with that intention – maybe even thinking of it as being appropriate for some child that he and Catherine were still hoping to have at that time. But behind the simple lyrics was a complex body of thought.

The pastoral imagery of the poems – they are full of lambs, flowers and children at play on the village green – can also be seen as a city-dweller's fantasy about the countryside. Blake was a townee, and there is little connection between his vision and the realities of rural life at the time. Yet we should not exaggerate the gap. Blake was no stranger to nature, despite being an impoverished inner-city dweller. In those days it was still possible to reach the country from Blake's native Soho by walking for twenty minutes northwards to the fields of Marylebone or westwards to those beyond Tyburn at the end of Oxford Street (or Oxford Road, as it was then called). However coloured by urban experience, Blake was frequently describing things he had seen with his own eyes. While many of the themes addressed are conventional to pastoral poetry, there were others that dealt with contemporary liberal concerns such as racial oppression ('The Little Black Boy') and child exploitation

17 *Illustration to Young's 'Night Thoughts': Night I, Page [3] c.*1795–7
Pen and water-colour
42 × 32.5
$(16\frac{1}{2} × 12\frac{3}{4})$
British Museum

Look what a fine morning it is. Insects,
Birds, & Animals, are all enjoying existence.

Published by J. Johnson, Sept.r 1.st 1791.

above left
18 *Songs of
Innocence:
Frontispiece* 1789
Relief etching with
watercolour
c.11.3 × 7.2
(4½ × 2⅞)
British Museum

above right
19 *'Look what a
fine morning it is':
Frontispiece to Mary
Wollstonecraft,
'Original Stories from
Real Life'* 1796
Engraving
13 × 6.5
(5⅛ × 2½)
Tate Gallery

('The Chimney Sweep'). At this point Blake was still aiming to celebrate the divine in all creation and tried to find good in situations where cruelty might seem to abound.

The *Songs of Experience* are a different matter. They were published four years later, in a changed world. The *Songs of Innocence* had been produced before the outbreak of the French Revolution when the hopes of the liberal- and progressive-minded for harmonious reform were high. *Experience* appeared at the height of the Terror, when France had become the prey of a tyrannical and paranoid government even crueller than that of the *ancien régime* and when the British Government had reacted with a panic lurch to the right and the introduction of repressive new laws. Many of the leading radicals such as Tom Paine had fled the country or fallen silent. Others, such as Fuseli, had changed their tune altogether and had become some- what jaundiced supporters of traditional values. Blake – already schooled in coping with failure by his experiences – had not rejected his earlier ideals. Instead he had deepened his perception of the problems that accom- panied them. He did not reject the songs of his innocent piper. He created a contrary for him in the form of the bard, who intones the *Songs of Experience*. The bard questions the themes of *Innocence* and provides alter- natives. The 'Blossom', which was a simple poem of delight in sexual love, is given the counterpart of the 'Rose' (fig.20) in which the beautiful flower is destroyed by the 'dark secret love' of the worm. The simple lamb dancing in the field is given the terrific counter-part of the 'Tyger, burning bright | In the forests of the night'. Attempts to make a good face of the horrifying treatment of chimney-sweeps are abandoned and the sweep in *Experience* has parents who devoutly pray in church while selling their son into appalling slavery (fig.21). The lyrical power is as strong as ever, but now it is expressing despair at the way in which cruelty and indifference flourish on all sides. Yet characteristic-ally for Blake, this despair, while recognising the hypocrisy of the world in which he lives, is not without hope. For he has an answer to the problem of why cruelty exists in a divinely created world. It is because that once-perfect world has fallen. This might seem to be the old story of the lost golden age – expressed in Christo-Judaic theology by the myth of the Garden of Eden. But it is not quite that. In that tradition the

20 *Songs of Experience: 'The Sick Rose'* 1794
Relief etching with watercolour
*c.*11.3 × 7.2
(4½ × 2⅞)
British Museum

burden of guilt lies on mankind. Mankind succumbed to the temptation of the Devil, ate the forbidden fruit and must therefore suffer. In Blake's cosmology the fault lies further back than that. It is the consequence of a cosmic split enforced by the authoritarian stance of the lawgiving Deity. Even the Devil who rebelled against this regime was not the cause of the problem. He was simply the first protester against oppression. While branded as wicked, the Devil was in fact life-affirming, full of the energy of eternal delight. By these means Blake keeps his doctrine of a rebellious assertion of individualism and experience alive. He did not buy the official story in religion any more than he did in politics or in society at large.

By presenting Innocence and Experience as two unresolved contraries Blake was keeping the debate open. Mortal existence comprised for him a seemingly endless pairing of such contraries – good and evil, male and female, reason and imagination, cruelty and kindness, Greek and Gothic ... all in their different ways indicating the split in existence that would even-tually, in his Messianic eyes, reach resolution. But such resolution could only be arrived at through a change in perception. The revolution had to be won first in the mind before it could triumph elsewhere.

This, essentially, is the message that lay behind the large cycle of illuminated texts that Blake was to produce over the next thirty years, using his own 'infernal method', printing them at home and colouring them with the assistance of Catherine. Before going on to discuss these, however, it might be helpful to look at the *Songs* again to consider the ways in which Blake uses words and images in combination in them. As has already been suggested, picture and poem can be likened to two voices, each performing its own part of the song. The word usually provides the lead, the image the harmonisation or accompaniment. But the image also changes the whole context of the word and makes it function in a different way. It turns a page into an integrated visual experience that may be taken in at one glance and then reflected upon. 'The Divine Image' in *Innocence* (fig. 22), for example, celebrates the godlike in Man. Blake adhered to the Christo-Judaic belief that God had created man in his own image, and that the human form was therefore the living embodiment of the Deity. The idea is inspiring. But the words, as you follow them line by line, move the eye downwards, a motion opposed to the uplifting effect of the message being revealed in the poem. To counteract this, Blake interwove the text with a flaming upward-moving organic shape that leads the eye back up the page and presents the emotion

21 *Songs of
Experience:
'The Chimney
Sweeper'* 1794
Relief etching with
watercolour
c.11.3 × 7.2
(4½ × 2⅞)
British Museum

22 *Songs of Innocence*: 'The Divine Image', 1789
Relief etching with watercolour
$c.11.3 \times 7.2$
$(4\frac{1}{2} \times 2\frac{7}{8})$
British Museum

in the poem as pure exhilaration. When colouring this form Blake endowed it with a magnificent golden hue to sing out against the deep blue of the page. Blake's illuminated books show a vivid sense of colour that was to strengthen as the years progressed, reaching its most magnificent expression in his last work, the watercolour illustrations to Dante (see figs. 57–9). 'The Divine Image' shows Blake using a flaming design for exhilarating effect. In 'The Sick Rose' in *Experience* he reverses the process. Here the sad story of the destructive power of love is conveyed pictorially by the downward curve of the sick rose's stem, which curls around the text and terminates in the blossom itself, bereft of support, reclining mournfully at the base of the page. The colours chosen for this design are sickly too, a murky green and bruised red. Not all connections between the verbal and visual operate as closely as this in the poems. Some have conventional structures. Some simply do not work. The innocuous pussy-cat that pads about at the base of 'The Tyger' can hardly be said to convey any of the 'fearful symmetry' of the beast that burns in the 'forests of the night' in the poem above its head (fig. 23).

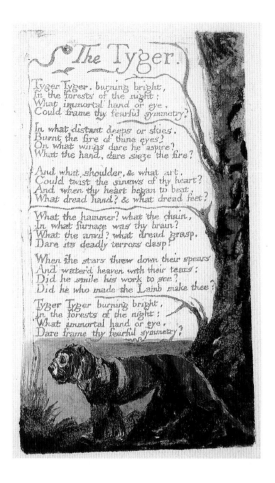

23 *Songs of Experience:
'The Tyger'* 1794
Relief etching with
watercolour
*c.*11.3 × 7.2
(4½ × 2⅞)
British Museum

Politics and Prophecy

By the time that *Songs of Experience* had been published a significant move
had taken place in Blake's life. He had left central London to live in what
was then the suburban region of Lambeth. From 1790 to 1800 he and his
wife occupied 13 Hercules Buildings. It was a modest house, but one that
had a garden and gave him a taste of near rural ease away from what
Mrs Blake called the 'terrible desart of London'.[2] In personal terms it was a
time of peace and seclusion. It may have been that Blake and his wife still
entertained thoughts at that time of starting a family – they were still both
in their thirties. It seems to have been a period of sensual pleasure and
delight. One visitor was surprised to call on them one day and find them
sitting completely naked in the garden, claiming to be Adam and Eve. Yet
professionally this was a time of growing darkness for Blake. His regular
publishing commissions were few and he was having to rely increasingly
on what seemed to be acts of near charity from his friends – such as the
request by Flaxman for a set of illustrations to the poet Thomas Gray for his
wife. Blake's reputation as a radical did not help his position. Indeed, it is
commonly thought that his move to Lambeth was made partly to avoid too

close a surveillance from those government agents increasingly bent on winkling out dangerous subversives in the volatile urban world. Despite this, however, Blake was active throughout this period publishing his prophetic books denouncing authority.

In these publications, which had begun in 1789 with the charming *Book of Thel* (fig. 24), Blake took issue with both conventional and radical politics and religion. One of the earliest, *The Marriage of Heaven and Hell* (see fig. 25), still uses the satirical form common amongst eighteenth-century rationalists. It is full of pithy, aphoristic statements. The title itself is a take-off of the topical religious tract *Heaven and Hell* by the Swedish spiritual leader Emanuel Swedenborg. Swedenborg – who founded a sect that still has its adherents today – had a great following amongst religious enthusiasts in London in the 1780s. Flaxman belonged to his church, and Blake and his wife also attended meetings of the Swedenborgians on more than one occasion. Like Blake, Swedenborg experienced visions, and related some of these in *Heaven and Hell*. But Blake felt in the end that Swedenborg was too bounded by conventional notions of good and evil. *The Marriage of Heaven and Hell* provides a 'contrary' to Swedenborg's view. Hell becomes for Blake the source of energy and delight, Heaven the seat of soulless lawgiving. Throughout the work there are memorable statements supporting individualism and freedom of thought and expression; 'One law for the Ox and the Lion is Oppression'; 'The fool sees not the same tree as the wise man.' There is also a series of 'memorable fancies', including one where Blake himself visits Hell and finds the source of the 'infernal method' that he had invented for his own kind of printing. The corrosives he used to etch out his words and design on the copperplate became likened to the cleansing vision that penetrates the detritus of daily life to expose the truth concealed below.

After *The Marriage of Heaven and Hell* Blake produced a series of prophetic books that attacked conventional morality and expounded his own Messianic view of world history. Each one addressed a particular problem. The following year, 1793, he published *Visions of the Daughters of Albion* (see fig. 26), which attacked the conventions of sexual morality, and in particular the double standards imposed on women. In the same year *America* was produced and then, in 1794, *Europe* (see figs. 1 and 2). These addressed different aspects of the current political turmoil.

These works should be the most clear and accessible of all, but in fact they are the most difficult and obscure. A key reason for this is because the narratives are peopled by mythological figures of Blake's own creation. The real and allegorical go hand in hand. In *America* Washington, Franklin and Paine share space with Orc and Oothoon, the two figures in Blake's mythology representing revolution and 'the soft soul of America' respectively.

It might well be asked why Blake did this. If he was issuing a prophetic message for the present, why did he obscure it all by peopling his narratives with these complex symbolic beings? One reason must surely be his understanding of the nature of myth. In his eyes myths encapsulated realities that could not be reached simply by cold reason. Blake was not alone in this

belief; since the middle of the century there had been a revival of interest in myth, as there had been in folk-songs and ballads. They were seen as embodying ancient wisdom. It was recognised increasingly that myths were not simply foolish tales invented by primitive people at whim, but that they were ways that had been used in the past for people to make sense of their experiences. Myth was the means of accounting for all that was incomprehensible in life, for the deep mysteries of how people had come into being, why they were here, why they had the feelings and desires that they did. This was the beginning of the understanding of myths as the bearers of deep psychological truths that has persisted into our own time. In the later eighteenth century many ancient mythologies were unearthed and published. Those of the Greeks and Romans had, of course, been known since antiquity. But these were joined by those of Northern Europe – such as could be found in the German *Nibelungenlied* and the Icelandic *Edda*. There were, as well, some notable spoofs. The most celebrated of these were the supposedly Gaelic poems of the ancient bard Ossian, published by James Macpherson in 1760 as *Fragments of Ancient Poetry Collected in the Highlands of Scotland*. These were already doubted by some in Blake's day, but he himself maintained a belief that they were, at the least, echoes of some archaic wisdom. In a sense Blake was trying to recover a mythology for Britain that had become lost, and thereby reintroduce an understanding of events that could not be grasped in any other way. He was also updating this world by bringing it into contact with the leaders and major events of his own times. Such remythologising was not unique to Britain. In Germany in particular it led to the *Kunstmärchen*, invented folk-tales such as Henry De La Motte Fouque's *Undine*, and the attempt to synthesise the myths of the ancient and modern worlds by the painter Philipp Otto Runge. Blake knew none of this when he began his own mythologising – though in later life he was to become an admirer of contemporary German literature. He made use of many of the same mystical sources as the German Romantics – the most important being that of the writings of the seventeenth-century shoemaker and visionary Jakob Boehme, known to Blake as 'Behmen'.

26 *Visions of the Daughters of Albion: 'The Argument'* c.1794–5 Relief etching with watercolour 8.1 × 11.2 $(3\frac{1}{4} \times 4\frac{3}{8})$ Fitzwilliam Museum, Cambridge

In his prophetic books Blake adopted an archaic tone – to a large extent actually based on the metre to be found in MacPherson's Ossianic sagas. The events in them are dramatic and elemental. The forms are gigantic and heroic – often naked or clad in diaphanous drapes. Gradually as they became used again and again they could be seen to represent spiritual states – such as Urizen, the judgemental father-figure limited by reason (see fig.27), or Los who stands for poetry and inspiration. It is a whole cosmology as imaginative and complex as that of any traditional mythology.

The prophetic books are really at the heart of Blake's thinking. For Blake scholars they are where he begins and ends. Undoubtedly this is true in terms of the profundity of his vision. His whole outlook was coloured by this mythical world that he created and his other productions can only be fully understood in the light of the ideas and actions that he worked out in his prophetic books. On the other hand, it would be wrong to assert that Blake's greatness lay only in these. Without the force of his poetic vision and the power of his imagery his mythical world would be of little interest to more than a handful of specialists. His claim to greater attention lies in his ability to grasp our imagination with the striking image and phrase, which can be seen at work in the most wonderful manner in the few lines that prefaced his unpublished poem 'Auguries of Innocence' which was apparently produced around 1803:

> To see a World in a Grain of Sand
> And a Heaven in a Wild Flower
> Hold Infinity in the Palm of your hand
> and Eternity in an hour.

His is not merely the ability to look at the minute and find the universe within it. This is a commonplace in mystical philosophies. It is the ability to grasp this with such vividness as to *see* in a grain of *sand* and to *hold* in the *palm* of your hand. These are very concrete and tangible images. They give form to abstract ideas. Blake makes the invisible visible, the intangible concrete.

Blake's insistence on his imagined world – and his seeing of visions – marked him out as an eccentric. On the whole, however, he was thought to be a harmless eccentric. After all, he was perfectly businesslike in his daily dealings, and while he could sometimes be a rather awkward, even cantankerous, customer, most people had no difficulty in conducting sane transactions with him. Possibly the image of him as a harmless madman saved him from the persecution that might have come his way had his message been more clearly understood. In 1793 an act was passed against 'divers wicked and seditious writings'.[3] There were many arrests during this period of national paranoia about subversive revolutionaries. Blake's writings were full of inflammatory ideas, but they did not attract the attention of the police. If he had attacked King George III outright he would almost certainly have ended up in jail. But as he railed against 'The Guardian Prince of Albion', nobody cared.

It is possible that Blake deliberately cultivated the image of eccentricity to evade censure. Possible, but doubtful. His use of mythology was too seriously related to his belief that this was the only way in which deeper truths could be expressed. He does, however, seem to have embraced the concept of madness. For he was one of those who had begun to see madness

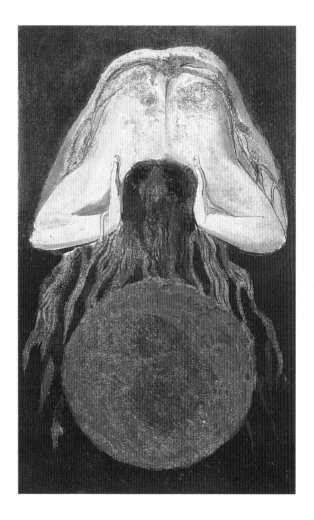

27 *Urizen, Plate 17*
1794
Relief etching with
watercolour
*c.*14.8 × 9
(5⅞ × 3½)
British Museum

not as derangement but as the perception of an alternative reality obscured to most 'normal' people: 'Cowper came to me and said: "O that I were insane always. I will never rest. Can you not make me truly insane? ... You retain health and yet are as mad as any of us – over us all – mad as a refuge from unbelief – from Bacon, Newton and Locke"'.[4] Blake is claiming here that his 'madness' preserves his vision against the blinkered perception of reason. It was an idea sufficiently fashionable at the time to aid the thin but continuous patronage he received.

Blake's prophecies were published in a spate of illuminated books during his early years in Lambeth up to 1795. After that the pace slowed down, although he continued to work on increasingly complex narratives and produced two further major epics – *Milton* (1803–c.1810) and *Jerusalem* (c.1804–c.1820). All these texts were illuminated, often with grand and powerful designs. At the same time, he had not abandoned his ambitions for his visual art to succeed in its own right. In 1795 he produced a series of twelve large prints which might be seen as an attempt to create a pictorial cycle to complement his verbal ones.

Like the illuminated books, the technique employed for these large prints – they are called the Lambeth prints because of the place of their origin – was a unique one. It was a form of colour printing. Essentially

28 Elohim creating Adam 1795
Colour print with watercolour and ink
42.1 × 53.6
($16\frac{5}{8} \times 21\frac{1}{4}$)
Tate Gallery

the process involved colouring up a piece of millboard and then taking a direct impression from it. The impressions were called monoprints because, in theory, only one printing could be made from each board. In practice, however, it seems Blake was usually able to take four or even five impressions. The image was then subsequently worked up. Lines were drawn over it in ink and watercolour additions were made to strengthen and sharpen the colour.

The themes of these prints – which appeared without any text – were not taken from Blake's own mythology, but were drawn from the Bible, Shakespeare and other major literary and historical sources. Many attempts have been made to read these images as a coherent group, or, alternatively, as a set of contraries; yet to date no completely convincing interpretation has been achieved. It seems clear, however, that they share the critical approach evident in his prophetic books, showing the effects of lack of vision, the tragedy of creation and the fallen state of the earth. All the images are negative. None are celebratory. Perhaps the most striking is the representation of *Elohim Creating Adam* (fig.28). In this the harsh Deity drags an unwilling Adam into being. It is the opposite of the humanistic – and traditional Judaic – concept of creation as a divine blessing. Blake would have known well the famous painting by his hero Michelangelo of God endowing man with the spark of life (see fig.29). His version of the event could almost be taken as a direct contrary to this. In *Nebuchadnezzar* (fig.30) he shows man having lost his senses – illustrating the biblical story of the Babylonian king who lapsed into madness after having persecuted the Jews. This subject had already been depicted by Mortimer in an engraving Blake would have known well, and Blake himself had used it in his *Marriage of Heaven and Hell*. Blake was inspired by the description in the Bible of how Nebuchadnezzar's 'hairs were grown like eagles' feathers and his nails like birds' claws'[5] to show the king literally becoming animal-like, his sinews seeming to sprout feathers and his feet growing claws. *Nebuchadnezzar* shows a man having lost his reason. *Newton* (fig.31) shows a man having lost everything but reason. He is satirised as a Grecian figure, looking downwards and measuring, unable to see the larger vision beyond. Blake's choice of Newton for this role was carefully calculated. The great scientist was the hero of the Enlightenment,

29 Buonarroti
Michelangelo
(1475–1564)
*Creation of Adam;
Sistine Chapel Ceiling*
1510
Fresco
The Vatican, Rome

who seemed more than any other to have explained the workings of nature through the application of experimental analysis and reason. Blake showed him as locked in limitation. For true understanding, in Blake's eyes, came only through vision and imagination.

The majority of the Lambeth prints focus on male figures. However, there are some female themes. In these the mood is softer – though the tone is equally dark. One shows a mysterious figure, possibly the witch Hecate, another a moving depiction of *Pity*, apparently inspired by verses from Macbeth that describe it '... like a naked new-borne babe, striding the blast ...' (fig.32).[6]

Blake's experiments with monoprints may have been encouraged by recent developments in colour printing. As the hand-colouring of his illuminated books shows, he was certainly convinced of the importance of colour by this date. He also appears to have enjoyed the special textural effects that could be created when the colours on the board were squashed against the paper. This helped to achieve the glimmering gloom common to the works and might have been inspired by the dark and dramatic work of his old acquaintance Henry Fuseli, in particular his *Nightmare*. Originally exhibited at the Royal Academy in 1782, this was repeated in several versions, the most striking being that now in Frankfurt, dated *c.*1791. Like Fuseli's *Nightmare*, the Lambeth prints depict powerful, gesturing figures in confined, darkened spaces.

above
30 *Nebuchadnezzar*
1795
Colour print with watercolour and ink
44.6 × 62
($17\frac{1}{2}$ × $24\frac{3}{8}$)
Tate Gallery

opposite top
31 *Newton c.*1795
Colour print with watercolour and ink
44.6 × 62
($17\frac{1}{2}$ × $24\frac{3}{8}$)
Tate Gallery

opposite bottom
32 *Pity c.*1795
Colour print with watercolour and ink
42.5 × 53.9
($16\frac{3}{4}$ × $21\frac{1}{4}$)
Tate Gallery

Fuseli and Darkness

As was seen earlier, Fuseli was the contemporary who was probably closest to Blake as an artist. Blake admired the fire and vigour of his art – even though he was aware of great differences of belief between them.

> The only Man that eer I knew
> Who did not make me almost spew
> was Fuseli he was both Turk and Jew
> And so dear Christians Friends how do you do[7]

Fuseli may have begun his career as a Zwinglian minister, but he had long lost any clear religious belief, and his art – while full of strong emotion – is without a sense of the spiritual. He explored the erotic in a carnal sense and his general approach to mythological and historical subjects might be said to have been psychological rather than spiritual. Blake had been close to Fuseli when they were both part of the circle of the radical publisher Joseph Johnson. They were clearly fascinated by each other as powerful and – in very different ways – aberrant figures. Fuseli was by far the more successful artist. Yet he recognised the potential force of Blake's images and commented once that he was 'damned good to steal from'.[8]

Blake undoubtedly found Fuseli's brilliant and destructive intellect exciting. The aphoristic statements in *The Marriage of Heaven and Hell*, created at the height of his intimacy with Fuseli, were inspired by the latter's iconoclastic sayings. In 1788 Blake had engraved a frontispiece, after Fuseli, for the *Aphorisms on Man* by the latter's Swiss associate Johann Caspar Lavater. Fuseli himself planned to publish a series of aphorisms on art as a counterpart to these. Such contraries must have been a further stimulus to Blake.

Yet intellectually and politically the differences between them were growing. Fuseli, a rationalist, was deeply shaken by the French Revolution and switched from being a radical to becoming a jaundiced conservative. It is possible that his return to the theme of *The Nightmare* around 1790 was a comment on his views of the nightmare that was unfolding in France at the time (interestingly Fuseli's *Nightmare* (fig.9) was adapted by satirical printmakers in France – usually to make jibes against frightened aristocrats). It is symptomatic of his changed mood that he accepted his election as a Royal Academician in 1790. In earlier years he had railed against the Academy as a promoter of mediocrity at the expense of genius. Now he took the pessimistic view that while academies could not promote innovative art they could at least preserve standards in a world where all seemed in decline.

The dark forces at play in Fuseli's art accorded with the then fashionable view of the Sublime in art. In 1757 a new reading of this term had been given by the Irish statesman Edmund Burke in his *Philosophical Enquiry into the Origins of our Ideas of the Sublime and Beautiful*. Taking a pragmatic view of the matter Burke argued that our sense of beauty was motivated by feelings of love, of the Sublime by feelings of fear. While this interpretation

33 *The Sun at His Eastern Gate (Milton's 'L'Allegro')* c.1816–20 Pen and watercolour 16 × 12.2 (6¼ × 4¾) Pierpont Morgan Library, New York

was much contested, it did sanction an aesthetic of fear. Blake, characteristically, was highly critical of Burke's understanding of the Sublime, since he saw the latter as being caused by an awareness of the Divine rather than by physical fear. He himself would present a far more uplifting vision of the Sublime – for example in his awe-inspiring image of *The Sun at His Eastern Gate* (fig. 33). But in his Lambeth prints he comes close to the Burkean view of the Sublime, since it is fear and foreboding that predominate – as in Fuseli's *Nightmare*. On the other hand, the iconography of these pictures makes clear that the fear comes from a lack of vision and understanding – a lack of vision that he could perceive, ultimately even in the powerful images of the one contemporary who did not make him 'almost spew'.

Blake's new, more energetic manner – so different from that used for his historical watercolours in the 1780s – was not limited to the Lambeth

34 *Glad Day or The Dance of Albion*, 1st engraved 1780, colour printed 1794–5 Engraving with watercolour 27.3 × 19.5 (10¾ × 7¾) British Museum

prints. At this time he looked back over some of his other images and remade some of them as more powerful works. *The Ancient of Days* was taken from its position as a frontispiece to *Europe* and turned into a free-standing print. He also adapted the image of Albion, originally intended for his history of England (fig. 34). He surrounded this figure rising to spiritual enlightenment with rainbow colours, suggesting that the Sublime could be about light as well as about darkness.

3

PATRONAGE AND PERSISTENCE

Flaxman and Friends

One of the reasons why Blake's production of prophetic books diminished so markedly around 1795 was financial. These books had brought in no money and Blake and his wife were now down to living on half a guinea a week – more or less the wages of a manual labourer of the day. Blake therefore turned to trying to revive his engraving career as well as his practice of making illustrations after other people's work. Many of his old friends were now established in their careers and they seem to have been behind most of the schemes of employment which came his way. Intensely proud, he would never have accepted charity from them. Yet it often seems that the commissions that he received were a kind of charity, given more out of friendship than out of real need. At the same time most of the larger commercial ventures that he undertook failed, usually because his work, while admired by some, was felt to be too strange to appeal to a general audience.

Blake, independent-minded as ever, was clear that he did not want the kind of patronage that had been dispensed to artists by the powerful in the past. 'Liberality! We want not Liberality,' he wrote against a part of Reynolds's *Discourses* that seemed particularly toadying in its adulation of noble munificence, 'We want a Fair Price and Proportionate Value & General Demand for Art.'[1] But these were just the things he could not get.

35 *Thomas Butts c.*1801
Watercolour on ivory
8.4 × 6.3 (3¼ × 2½)
British Museum

Blake's patrons and supporters were, hardly surprisingly, rarely of the aristocratic kind. They tended to be fellow artists and publishers, on the one hand, and modest gentlemen with rather eccentric tastes on the other. Foremost amongst the first group were the sculptor Flaxman and the painter John Linnell. Foremost amongst the second was Thomas Butts (see fig. 35), a minor civil servant who became Blake's most constant source of employment for nearly twenty years from 1797 onwards.

From the time that Flaxman returned from Rome in 1794 he had concerned himself with the well-being of his former fellow student. Artistically, Flaxman provided the Heaven to Fuseli's Hell for Blake. The satanic Fuseli, full of energy and passion, attracted Blake artistically more than the saintly Flaxman. But Fuseli was relatively disparaging about him in private conversation. 'Fuseli has known him for several years', wrote the

36 *Thomas Gray's Poems: 'The Progress of Poesy', page 6*
*c.*1797–8
Watercolour
*c.*42 × 32.5
($16\frac{1}{2}$ × $12\frac{1}{4}$)
Yale Center for British Art, Paul Mellon Collection

38 After William Blake,
Death's Door by L. Schiavonetti 1805
Engraving 27.3 × 15.5 (10¼ × 6⅛)
British Museum

37 *'Group of Negros,
as imported to be sold
for Slaves', from
Stedman, 'Narrative of
a Five Years'
Expedition, against the
Revolted Negros of
Surinam' 1796*
Engraving
British Library

Royal Academician Joseph Farington about Blake in 1796, 'and thinks he
has a great deal of invention, but that "fancy is the end not the means in his
designs". He does not employ it to give novelty and decoration to regular
inventions.'[2] Fuseli's reference to fancy being the 'end not the means' in
Blake's art draws the distinction with himself, enough of an academic now
to think of his work as 'art' first and 'meaning' second. Perhaps Fuseli was
disparaging about Blake to safeguard his own position, for it might seem to
some that his own fantasies came dangerously close to those of the mad,
proletarian radical at times.

Flaxman, gentle, well-behaved and a devout Swedenborgian, seemed to
represent in Blake's mind all that he had criticised in *The Marriage of Heaven
and Hell*. He epitomised the lawgiving, rule-obeying side of goodness.
Doubtless he saw helping Blake as part of his Christian duty. Blake, who
must have been aware of this, did not always behave with the correct
degree of gratitude. He did not take the receipt of charity well, and always
insisted on any transactions being conducted strictly on business terms.
Over the years Flaxman put all kinds of business Blake's way – including
the engraving of illustrated catalogues for the potter Josiah Wedgwood.

Perhaps most galling of all was Flaxman's seeming indifference to Blake's
true artistic identity. It is a common feature of all Blake's patrons that they

did not commission him to illuminate his own work or ideas, but the works of others. In 1797 Flaxman commissioned Blake to produce a set of 116 watercolours to the poems of the fashionable poet Thomas Gray for his wife Nancy. The resultant work – which was delivered some time before September 1805 – adopts the light tone of Gray's work but also sends it up to some degree (see fig. 36). Blake's method for this illustrative work was to provide broad border decorations – a parody of the illumination that he had provided for his own prophetic books, just as the style is a parody of Gray. This commission came hard on the heels of a more ambitious scheme for illustrating the masterpiece of Edward Young, another famous nature poet of the time. Young's *Night Thoughts* were commissioned by Richard Edwards, a publisher who admired Blake's work and had used him to engrave other designs such as Captain Stedman's *Narrative* of the Negro rebellion in Surinam (fig. 37). Stedman was one of the 'eccentric gentlemen' whom Blake had contact with at this time. Although he did not share Stedman's political views, he took the illustration of his narrative as a means of expressing concern at the appalling conditions of slavery still prevalent at that time.

Blake made no fewer than 537 watercolours for Young – but the project failed, leaving him with little financial reward. A final ignominy occurred in 1805 when the publisher Robert Cromek commissioned illustrations to a further fashionable poem, Robert Blair's *The Grave* (fig. 15). Cromek

became disconcerted by Blake's severe style and turned the actual engraving of the plates over to the popular engraver Luigi Schiavonetti (see fig. 38). There was a further breakdown of relations when Cromek commissioned the successful painter Thomas Stothard to design a picture of Chaucer's Canterbury pilgrims – an idea that Blake appears to have had originally proposed. In fury Blake persisted with his own design and subsequently engraved it (fig. 39).

Hayley's Arcadia

Flaxman's circle of friendship and influence was wide. He seems to have been behind the arrangement for Blake to abandon his toe-hold on the London art world altogether and go to Felpham in Sussex where he fell under the patronage of the minor poet and minor gentleman William Hayley. Hayley was moderately successful as a poet, and was a man of independent means and generous disposition. Somewhat eccentric in his own behaviour, he made a habit of befriending unbalanced people of talent. One of the first was the neurotic painter George Romney. His best-known was the 'mad' poet William Cowper, for whom he secured a pension. Flaxman seems to have introduced Hayley to Blake at a moment when Cowper had recently died and when Hayley had almost simultaneously suffered the grief of losing his brilliant, illegitimate son at the age of 20. He

40 *Heads of the Poets: Cowper*
*c.*1800–3
Tempera on canvas
41.9 × 83.6
(16½ × 32⅞)
Manchester City Art Galleries

undoubtedly saw Blake as his next good cause and in 1800 persuaded him to move to Sussex, where he lived for three years.

Blake's time at Felpham – where he had his own cottage – began with great enthusiasm. Hayley provided work for him – commissioning him to provide illustrations for his works and a series of heads of great poets for his library (see fig.40). He also found employment for him from local gentry, taught him Greek and encouraged him to develop as a painter of miniatures. But in the end Blake became irritated. This was partly because Hayley – a greatly inferior if more successful poet – appeared to have no understanding or appreciation of Blake's own visionary writing, and partly because he expected to run Blake's life. Hayley's great generosity towards those neurotic, creative individuals that he came to protect can be seen as a need to be rewarded and loved. He was deeply offended and upset when Blake wished to assert himself – and particularly by Blake's implication that Hayley was stifling him and preventing him from realising his next great prophetic works, *The Four Zoas* and *Milton*. 'O God, protect me from my friends, that they have not power over me', Blake later complained in *Milton*.[3]

Hayley's presence became too suffocating and Blake determined to return to London and poverty. But this did not occur before one incident which nearly undid him altogether. One night he ejected a drunken soldier from his garden. This man, Private John Scolfield, brought a charge of treason against Blake for supposedly having cursed the King. The case was tried at Chichester and might well have succeeded had not Hayley been tireless in his support of his former protégé. Blake was deeply aware of the great generosity of this move. But this did not prevent him from representing Hayley in a derogatory manner in *Milton*. With considerably more justice Scolfield was turned into the villainous Accuser in *Jerusalem*.

The Return

In September 1803 Blake moved back to London; he and his wife were never to leave it again. They settled first in South Molton Street, close to Blake's brother in Broad Street, and finally, in 1820, in Fountain Court, just off the Strand. Blake was returning to the scenes of his childhood, and to his status as a lowly craftsman. By the early nineteenth century most of the artistic community was separating itself from that of craftsmen, physically as well as socially. Fine artists now lived in the new houses being erected north of Oxford Street in the area between Regent Street and Tottenham Court Road – what later became known as Fitzrovia. This is where Benjamin West (now President of the Royal Academy), Flaxman and Fuseli lived, as well as artists of the younger generation such as Constable. Blake remained on the south side of Oxford Street, in the confined inner-city environment of the craftsman.

For the next six years Blake struggled to re-establish himself in the commercial practice he had had before his exodus to the country. Work for publishers was harder to come by now – partly because of the setback to the printing trade caused by the Continental Blockade. His quarrel with the publisher Cromek over his design for *The Canterbury Pilgrims* made an enemy, on the way, of Thomas Stothard, an Academician who had previously been amongst his supporters. He even fell out with Flaxman for a time, and finally, at the end of this period, was losing the patronage of his most stalwart supporter, Thomas Butts.

This period of increasing material disaster was, however, one of strengthening artistic and visionary resolve. In *Milton*, the poem that he was working on between 1803 and 1810, he described his vision as having been renewed.

History Painting and Exhibition

While reverting to his prophetic writing, Blake was also reviving his ambition to succeed as a history painter. In a way the spectacular series of Lambeth prints had already signalled this. It was from this process that he devised a new technique for historical works. Termed by him 'tempera' – or even on occasion 'fresco' – it involved the application of paint using carpenter's glue as a binding medium. It was supposed to be a reconstruction of the painting techniques used by early Italian artists and was considered by Blake to be significantly different from oil painting, the technique normally used for painting in the period. Blake associated oil with sensuality and materialism – its ability to suggest rich textures and fabrics leading artists away from the severe delineation of line and form. His espousal of the more primitive techniques of tempera and fresco led back to a time before the materialist modern age when the primitive forms of works were made clear. Blake was fortunate in finding in Thomas Butts (1757–1845) a patron who was willing to support him in such work. Butts, a Swedenborgian, was probably another of Flaxman's contacts. Blake became so enthused by his support that he addressed him in a letter of 1800 as 'Dear Friend of My Angels'.[4] Butts was a clerk in the office of the Commissary General of Musters; for nearly twenty years he supported Blake, paying him a retainer for much of the time. Early in their relationship, Blake produced a series of fifty temperas on biblical themes for Butts. One, *The Miracle of the Loaves and Fishes*, was exhibited at the Royal Academy in 1800. It was a further sign that he was intending to return to history painting.

41 *Jacob's Dream*
*c.*1800–3
Watercolour
37 × 29.2
($14\frac{5}{8} \times 11\frac{1}{2}$)
British Museum

Blake continued to paint in tempera until his last years, but on the whole he used watercolour for commissioned work. This was the medium in which he worked for Butts after the first tempera series (see figs.41–3). Watercolour was a more conventional and more manageable technique. Blake could content himself, moreover, with the thought that it was closer to fresco than oil painting was (indeed, he claimed in his descriptive catalogue that it essentially *was* fresco). Like fresco, watercolour was a light medium. It could combine well with hard outline drawing and the use of bright, vibrant colours.

Blake's use of watercolour, while being justified on grounds of archaism, was also highly contemporary and innovative, for this was the period in which watercolour became a British speciality. From being employed simply as a way of making 'coloured drawings', it began to be used for achieving purely painterly effects. This revolution was being achieved by

42 *God Blessing
the Seventh Day*
*c.*1805
Watercolour
42 × 35.5
(16½ × 14)
private collection

43 *The Great
Red Dragon and
the Woman
Clothed with the
Sun c.*1806–9
Watercolour
43.5 × 34.5
(17⅛ × 13⅝)
Brooklyn
Museum of Art,
New York, Gift
of William A.
White

brilliant young artists such as Turner and Girtin at precisely the time that Blake was beginning to focus on watercolour as one of his main forms of pictorial expression. It is not known what, if any, contact Blake had with such artists. He did not partake in the founding of the Watercolour Society in 1804; but he did show at the breakaway *Associated Painters in Water-Colour* in 1812. It must be remembered, too, that the use of watercolour was always something of a compromise for Blake. Ideally he would have liked to have been at work producing vast murals in fresco.

The largest part of the work that Blake produced for Butts consisted of illustrations to Milton (see fig.44). The impetus for this probably came more from Blake than from Butts, who was a very indulgent patron. Blake was also producing Miltonic pictures for other patrons, such as the Reverend Joseph Thomas. Doubtless Blake was inspired by his own literary engagement with Milton, expressed in his epic poem of that title. He may have been stimulated, too, by a sense of rivalry with Fuseli. Fuseli, during the 1790s, had been constructing a Milton Gallery – itself an emulation of Boydell's Shakespeare Gallery. The outcome was a financial disaster for Fuseli, but the venture probably stimulated Blake to think about Milton as a source for visual as well as verbal inspiration. Many of Blake's water-colours engage with Milton's retelling of biblical stories. Some of the most beautiful describe Christ's crucifixion and resurrection. A particularly moving one shows two angels watching over the body of the dead Christ, their wings touching to form a Gothic arch (fig.45). Blake himself must have been particularly pleased with this design as it is one of a handful of

44 *Adam and Eve Asleep* 1808 Watercolour 49.2 × 38.8 ($19\frac{3}{8} \times 15\frac{1}{4}$) Museum of Fine Arts, Boston. Gift by Subscription 1890

works that he exhibited at the Royal Academy in 1808. It shows the superb sense of design that underlies his best work. The image is symmetrical. It is not the fearful symmetry of the Tyger, however, but rather one that suggests, in a way that inspires awe, a hidden order behind the visible.

Blake showed three watercolours at the Royal Academy exhibition of 1808, including the magnificent *Vision of the Last Judgement* that he had painted for the Countess of Egremont (fig.46). He may have thought the time was right for him to succeed as a history painter. Certainly the auguries were more favourable than they had been in the earlier period. Unlike Reynolds, Benjamin West, the current President of the Royal Academy, was one of his admirers. Furthermore he now had friends such as Fuseli and Flaxman amongst the ranks of the

45 *Christ in the Sepulchre, Guarded by Angels c.*1805. Watercolour 42.2 × 31.4 (16⅝ × 12⅜)
Courtesy of the Trustees of the Victoria and Albert Museum, London

Academicians. History painting was also receiving some public encouragement at this time, largely for patriotic reasons. Britain was back at war with France and it was felt appropriate that a British school of history painters should be encouraged both to commemorate the heroes of the conflict and to provide a pictorial alternative to the 'corrupt' work of the French Neoclassical painter David and his followers.

Emboldened by such signs, Blake decided in 1809 to stage a one-man show. This was held at the house of his elder brother James in Golden Square. The exhibition was accompanied by a *Descriptive Catalogue* in which he gave detailed accounts of his subjects and his ideas. Seemingly in preparation for this he had started reading the *Discourses* of Reynolds, making acerbic comments in the margins of his copy.

46 *The Vision of the Last Judgement* 1808
Watercolour
51 × 39.5
(20⅛ × 15½)
The National Trust Photographic Library

He shared many of Reynolds's ideals – in particular the elevated view of history painting. But he took exception to Reynolds's urbaneness and rationalism. Reynolds thought that art could be learned, and that the ideal could be discovered as a kind of norm created from the generalising of the characteristics of the individual forms found in nature. 'To generalize is to be an idiot', was Blake's response. His overall opinion about Reynolds was that 'This Man was Hired to Depress Art'.[5] It was a view that was to be shared increasingly by others. Within a few years the critic William Hazlitt was to be attacking Reynolds's generalisations about art with every bit as much vehemence as Blake.

Blake included many of his biblical and Miltonic subjects amongst the items in his exhibition. He also showed works more directly relevant to the war effort. The most remarkable of these were the *Spiritual Form of Nelson* (fig.47) and the *Spiritual Form of Pitt*. These commemorated the two great leaders who had recently died; the naval hero of Trafalgar and the prime minister who had succeeded in keeping Napoleon in check. These allegories (particularly that of Nelson, who is shown nude) might seem to be amazing liberties. But we should remember that allegorising the famous dead was a commonplace in high art. Just a couple of years earlier Benjamin West had designed an apotheosis of Nelson that showed him wafted heavenwards in a drape, being received by Britannia and assorted symbolic entities (fig.48). Blake may well have seen this when it was exhibited at West's house in 1807. Although West himself later veered away from such work, apotheoses were very popular at the time. In France the painter

A.-L. Girodet conceived an image that showed Napoleonic generals being received by the heroes of Ossian in heaven.[6] Blake's naked Nelson – holding apart the coils of Leviathan, the biblical monster of the deep, like a circus strongman – was no more inherently absurd than these.

Unfortunately for Blake his exhibition did not meet with the success that he had hoped. Dismissed as a 'farrago of nonsense' by Robert Hunt in the *Examiner*, the only journal that reviewed it, it went almost unnoticed elsewhere. There was, however, one revealing side-effect. The lawyer and journalist Henry Crabb Robinson, who had recently returned from Germany, saw the show and was impressed, from his reading of the *Descriptive Catalogue*, by how close Blake's ideas were to those of the German philosophers, poets and painters that he had been in contact with. As a result he wrote an article on Blake for the Hamburg magazine *Vaterländisches Museum*. This was the first publication on Blake ever to appear. Unfortunately it had no impact in Britain whatsoever. There is an

47 *The Spiritual Form of Nelson Guiding Leviathan* c.1809
Tempera on canvas
76.2 × 62.5
(30 × 24⅜)
Tate Gallery

even more intriguing twist: one of the artists whose work most resembled that of Blake was the Hamburg-based painter Philipp Otto Runge, then working on his mystical allegory *The Times of Day* (fig.49). Runge was a friend of the publisher and editor of the *Vaterländisches Museum*, Friedrich Perthes, and had designed a symbolic cover for the journal that has a Blakean flavour about it. But Runge was dead by the time the issue containing the article on Blake actually appeared. In all probability he never knew about it. Blake, for his part, knew nothing of Runge. Indeed, he did not even meet Crabb Robinson until the 1820s. So the work that would seem to have been bringing these two visionary artists into contact with each other in practice did nothing of the sort.

The failure of the special exhibition may have drawn a line under Blake's professional ambitions as a history painter. But he did not abandon such work. He exhibited his *Apotheosis* of *Pitt* and of *Nelson* at the *Associated Painters in Watercolour* in 1812. He continued to work in tempera when the occasion allowed, and produced some of his finest works in this medium – such as, in the 1820s, *The Body of Abel Found by Adam and Eve* (fig.3). He also persisted with his Miltonic watercolours – producing the marvellous illustrations to *L'Allegro* and *Il Penseroso*, probably for Butts, some time after 1816 (see fig.33). These later Miltonic subjects are far more colourful than the early ones. Blake discovered increasingly in later life the emotive power of colour.

above left
48 Benjamin West
(1738–1820)
The Immortality of Nelson 1807
Oil on canvas
100.3 × 64.8
(39$\frac{1}{2}$ × 25$\frac{1}{2}$)
National Maritime Museum Greenwich

above right
49 Philipp Otto Runge
(1777–1810)
The Times of Day: Night 1803
Pen and pencil
95.2 × 62.7
(37$\frac{1}{2}$ × 24$\frac{3}{4}$)
Hamburger Kunsthalle

THE PATRIARCH

Jerusalem and Redemption

It is always something of a disappointment to learn that those stirring verses beginning 'And did those feet' and ending with the building of 'Jerusalem in England's green and pleasant land' don't actually come from *Jerusalem* but from *Milton*. On the other hand, this shows a continuity of concern. Blake, in his last two great epic poems, was engaging with a spiritual regeneration that was both personal and public. It encompassed both his own spiritual struggle with the inheritance of England's greatest epic poet and the history of Britain.

In Blake's mythology Jerusalem is the 'emanation' (that is, the female counterpart) of Albion, the symbolic personification of Britain. *Jerusalem*, his longest and most complex poem, charts the history of their separation, and the evils that arise from this. It ends with the reunification of both in one perfect, bisexual being, and the re-establishment of eternal bliss at the end of time.

Comprising 100 plates of densely written text, this book is less decorative than some of Blake's. However, it is punctuated by significant images, such as that of the lovers embracing in the lily at the head of chapter 2 (fig.50). Sexual love was for Blake an image of the more perfect bliss that was to come in paradise. It was one of those harbingers of beauty and joy that could uplift us in the fallen world. He saw the regulation of sex within society as one of the most telling indicators of the repression brought about by the forces of reason.

Jerusalem can be read in personal terms, as the progress of a soul towards enlightenment. However, the poem also had a public side and addressed a contemporary situation. For most of the period in which Blake was writing the poem Britain was embroiled in war with France. It was also expanding in terms of industrial strength, wealth and imperial power. When Britain emerged as the victor at the battle of Waterloo there began a prolonged period in which it was the most powerful nation in the world and saw itself as the arbiter of international affairs. Many at the time argued that this was a natural destiny. Such apologists as the historian and lawyer Sharon Turner, in his highly popular *History of the Saxons*,[1] argued that this was the natural outcome of the resilience of the Anglo-Saxons, allied with advantages provided by the revealed religion of Protestantism. Great Britain – that political union of countries that had been forged in the eighteenth century – was seen as the triumphant outcome of this emergent process, in which the Anglo-Saxon Protestant element predominated.[2]

In one sense Blake's *Jerusalem* can be seen as an allegorical version of this

Jerusalem.
Chap: 2.

Every ornament of perfection. and every labour of love.
In all the Garden of Eden. & in all the golden mountains
Was become an envied horror. and a remembrance of jealousy:
And every Act a Crime. and Albion the punisher & judge

And Albion spoke from his secret seat and said

All these ornaments are crimes. they are made by the labours
Of loves: of unnatural consanguinities and friendships
Horrid to think of when enquired deeply into; and all
These hills & valleys are accursed witnesses of Sin
I therefore. condense them into solid rocks. stedfast:
A foundation and certainty and demonstrative truth:
That Man be separate from Man, & here I plant my seat.

Cold snows drifted around him: ice covered his loins around
He sat by Tyburns brook, and underneath his heel shot up!
A deadly Tree, he namd it Moral Virtue, and the Law
Of God who dwells in Chaos hidden from the human sight.

The Tree spread over him its cold shadows. (Albion groand)
They bent down, they felt the earth and again enrooting
Shot into many a Tree: an endless labyrinth of woe!

From willing sacrifice of Self, to sacrifice of (miscalld) Enemies
For Atonement: Albion began to erect twelve Altars,
Of rough unhewn rocks: before the Potters Furnace
He namd them Justice, and Truth. And Albions Sons
Must have become the first Victims. being the first transgressors
But they fled to the mountains to seek ransom: building A Strong
Fortification against the Divine Humanity and Mercy
In Shame & Jealousy to annihilate Jerusalem

50 *Jerusalem: Chapter 2, Page 28, 'Lovers in a Lily'*
*c.*1820
Relief etching and white-line engraving
22.1 × 16
(8¼ × 6¼)
Yale Center for British Art, Paul Mellon Collection

story. The story of Albion and Jerusalem encompasses world history. The process of the spiritual fall and regeneration is presented as both beginning and ending in Britain. There is a clear patriotic element here – something that made it possible for the verses about Jerusalem from *Milton* to be turned into an alternative national anthem when set to music by Parry during World War One. On the other hand, Blake's presentation of the matter is hardly a vindication either of imperialism or Protestant ascendancy. He sees 'England' as a union of races forged together by Los, his image of the creative spirit: 'What do I see. The Briton, Saxon, Roman, Norman amalgamating in my Furnaces into One Nation, the English.'[3]

While his visionary individualism can be seen in broad terms as part of a Protestant mystical tradition, Blake does not privilege Protestants in his envisioned spiritual re-unification. Rather he sees Protestantism as one of the divisive forces that has bred war and dissent in world history: 'Remember how Calvin and Luther in fury premature sow'd War and stern division between Papists and Protestants. Let it not be so now! go not forth in Martyrdoms and Wars!'[4]

Blake's use of the term 'English' to represent this union might be questioned nowadays. But this should not lead us to misunderstand the character of the broader union that he was envisioning. In his narrative he gave significant weight to the pre-Saxon history of Britain and took a strong interest in the traditions of the Druids and the Ancient Britons. Perhaps most important of all is the way that he saw division as a consequence of the false materialism of the present with all its greed and aggression. Redemption involved sharing, not domination.

The New Generation

Having delivered himself of *Jerusalem*, Blake seemed content to accept the role of patriarch. Now in his sixties, he had the pleasure of seeing his work taken up and venerated by a new generation. Unlike his earlier supporters, these younger enthusiasts were not condescending.

The change in attitude was partly a result of broader changes in the art world. The concept of the artist as a spiritual leader had prospered, and those elements that had made Blake seem fatally eccentric to an earlier generation could now be viewed more positively. Even given this change, however, he must be counted fortunate to have been introduced by his old friend and patron George Cumberland to John Linnell (1792–1882), the artist who did more than anyone else to ease his life in his later years, and to stimulate him to produce some last great works. He also produced one of the most attractive portraits of Blake – a sketch of him on a visit to Hampstead Heath (see frontispiece).

Linnell was to become as important to Blake in these last years as Butts had been in the previous two decades. Like Butts he paid Blake a retainer while the latter was producing work for him. Blake had, as we have already seen, always been suspicious of and hostile to the notion of patronage. Yet he worked for Linnell apparently without problem. Linnell seems in this sense to have fallen between Butts and Hayley. Butts, as far as can be seen, would commission the works Blake wanted to do with little demur. Hayley tried to dictate. Linnell placed orders for copies of books and pictures that Blake had already made, such as *The Wise and Foolish Virgins*, originally designed for Butts (fig. 51). But he also guided him towards new ventures. His two major commissions – the engravings of *Job* and the illustrations to *Dante* – were both master-strokes. They led to the production of works that simultaneously showed Blake's qualities as a visual artist at their height and had a genuinely broad appeal.

Blake may have been more willing to be guided at this time than previously because he had now reached the end of his great prophetic cycle. After *Jerusalem* had been published he wrote little new poetical work. It might also have been because his financial position was particularly

51 *The Parable of the Wise and Foolish Virgins* c.1822
Watercolour
36.3 × 33.7
($14\frac{1}{4}$ × $13\frac{1}{4}$)
Fitzwilliam Museum, Cambridge

desperate. His poverty was such that he had been forced to sell off his fine collection of prints – that vital source of imagery that he had been accumulating with such care since boyhood. In the same year (1820) he moved to Fountain Court where he spent the last seven years of his life, living with his wife in two rooms. The arrangement was still professional. One room was kept for the 'shop', where visitors and clients were received, and the other had to make do for all other purposes – workshop, kitchen, bedroom and living-room.

Blake's tendency to be accommodating to Linnell may also have resulted from finding through him the first group of artists who wholeheartedly admired his work, without the caveats and hesitations that even Fuseli and Flaxman had expressed. This group was very much younger, in their twenties and early thirties – the generation of Keats, Byron and Shelley. Like these great poets they were able to accept the notion of the artist as a visionary and political activist. They had little interest in the politeness of fine art.

It is striking that these young artists – Linnell, John Varley, Samuel Palmer, Edward Calvert and George Richmond – had a strong attachment to landscape painting. For some it was their major practice. This might seem strange, since landscape was not Blake's forte. Indeed, his pronouncements against 'natural religion' would seem to make him sceptical of the genre as being one bound to the material rather than the spiritual world. But this was landscape as it had been practised in the eighteenth century and not as it was perceived by the generation of Keats and Shelley. It had been the earlier poets Wordsworth and Coleridge (still juniors to Blake) who had made the great breakthrough in the poetic apprehension of nature to align the imagery of the outer world with the movements of the soul. In parallel to them artists such as Turner and Girtin had evolved a new form of landscape in which subjective apprehension became the centre of the art making it possible to sense the infinite in the mists of common day. As Blake put it, 'a fool sees not the same tree as a wise man sees'.[5]

These younger landscape painters were heirs to a vision-laden type of landscape that came much closer to the Blakean perception of the divine in all creation. Blake had, after all, filled his poetry with nature imagery, but it had always been nature perceived from the visionary angle, and this is what attracted the younger generation of landscapists. Thus, while figurative artists were on the whole unable to perceive the full dimensions of Blake's vision, landscape painters of this age accepted it with enthusiasm.

Blake, on his side, was prepared to be accommodating to his young admirers. Extreme examples of this are the 'Visionary Heads' that he drew

52 *The Man who Taught Blake Painting in his Dreams*
*c.*1819–20
Pencil
30 × 24.5 (11¾ × 9⅜)
Fitzwilliam Museum,
Cambridge

for John Varley (1778–1842). Varley was a landscape watercolourist. He was also an astrologer who produced a *Treatise on Zodiacal Physiognomy* in 1828. He believed that Blake's visions were literal occurrences. Blake would sit up in Varley's house all night drawing figures from the past who appeared before him (see fig.52). It seems almost certain that Blake was humouring Varley in this case, treating images that emerged inside his own mind as though they were projected before him. The result was a series of remarkable heads of historical and imaginary personages. Not all were human. On one of these occasions Blake made three sketches of *The Ghost of a Flea*, which he later worked up into a tempera painting (fig.4).

Blake's Pastoral

It was through Linnell's good offices that Blake was commissioned to provide wood-engravings for a school edition of Virgil's *Eclogues*, Dr Robert Thornton's *The Pastorals of Virgil* (see fig.53). These vivid engravings horrified Thornton, and he only went ahead with including them in his book after they had been vouched for by Sir Thomas Lawrence, the new President of the Royal Academy. Like West before him, Lawrence was an admirer of Blake and actually owned some of his work.

Blake's part in Thornton's project was a very minor one. He was not given any of Virgil's actual *Eclogues* to illustrate but was relegated instead to embellishing one of the imitations of Virgil by the eighteenth-century English poet Ambrose Phillips. Despite this, Blake used the occasion to develop a new kind of pastoral picture. That he could now consider landscape in visionary terms is perhaps a tribute to Linnell and his associates. Blake also had some sympathy with the aims of Thornton, despite the latter's incomprehension of his work. For Thornton had included illustrations in his *Pastorals* in the belief that telling images would help to fix the subject-matter and even the language of Virgil in students' minds. For this reason he wanted the pictures to be right beside the actual piece of text that they illustrated. Blake, who had spent his life aligning word and image, was able to respond to this challenge admirably. Some of the engravings accompany single phrases, such as 'the blighted corn' or 'the briny ocean turns to pastures dry'. The features of these landscapes – the moons, trees, rivers and crops – are magnified, their

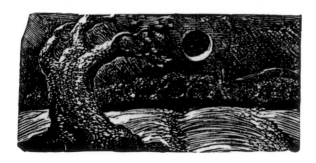

53 *Illustrations to Thornton's 'The Pastorals of Virgil': The Blighted Corn* 1821/*c.*1830 Wood engraving 3.4 × 7.3 ($1\frac{1}{4}$ × $2\frac{7}{8}$) Tate Gallery

distinctness emphasised as though they had become words, each with its own symbolic charge.

Much of the controversy over Blake's illustrations related to the technique he used for them. In wood-engraving, lines cut in the block come out as white or blank areas in the final print. This is the inverse of conventional drawing, or indeed of copper-engraving, where marks made on the page or plate emerge as dark or positive lines. At the time Blake was working it was habitual to make the wood-engraving simulate the effect of the drawing or copper print. This was done by means of a laborious process whereby a line was achieved by gouging out the block to either side of it, leaving a ridge standing that would produce a black or positive line in the final print. Blake ignored this practice and cut his lines as positive whites. The conventional engravers engaged in the rest of the book were outraged at this apparent ignorance of their craft and one even did some demonstration blocks in the conventional manner to show how they should be cut. Fortunately, because of Lawrence's intervention, Thornton agreed to leave the blocks as cut by Blake, only adding an apologetic note in the book that Blake's blocks 'display less art than genius, and are much admired by some eminent painters'. In fact, Blake's method of cutting white on black is critical for giving the images that sense of low, glimmering light which is central to their appeal, and, indeed, to the expression of a rich, dark pastoral so much more profound than the normal images of sporting nymphs and shepherds. Blake's method had a critical influence in the early twentieth century on revivers of wood-engraving such as Paul Nash and Robert Gibbons.

Interpreting Job

Another project instigated by Linnell was the engraving and elaboration of the illustrations that Blake had made to the Book of Job for Thomas Butts. This emerged from a set of commissions that Linnell had been making for Blake to copy various works he had done for Butts, largely from the Bible and from Milton. It is not clear what encouraged him to make the bold step of financing Blake to execute a set of engravings after the Job series, but his shrewd business instincts no doubt gave him a sense that this was something in which Blake might be able to succeed commercially. The biblical story was well known and, while it contained a mystical element, it was accessible in a way that Blake's own subject-matter rarely was. It also had a happy ending. After having endured the tribulations brought upon him by the Devil with his faith unimpaired, Job is rewarded by God with the restoration of his health, wealth and family.

When making these engravings Blake kept fairly faithfully to his original watercolour designs. However, he adopted the unusual process of framing each picture with a broad border containing outline designs and texts. It was in a sense a reversal of his normal illumination process, in which the text was surrounded by imagery, but in this case he was being a commentator on himself, on a series of pictures he had already created.

The technical process used was that of conventional line-engraving. Yet some of the effect of having worked with wood-engraving seems to have stayed with Blake, for the plates have a far more textured look than his earlier line-engravings and share something of the glimmering light effects achieved in the *Pastorals* illustrations.

Blake was keen to provide a commentary on his illustrations presumably because he wanted to emphasise – as ever – his own interpretation of the story. In the Bible Job is rewarded for having sustained his faith under tribulation. Blake revised this to suggest that Job was being recompensed because, after tribulation, he now understood the nature of faith in a more profound manner than before. A comparison between the opening and closing plates makes this clear. In the first scene (fig.54) Job and his family pray in a conventional manner. The children kneel, the patriarch and his wife are seated with books on their laps. A church is seen, its spire silhouetted against the setting sun in the background. 'Thus did Job continually' is written conspicuously beneath the scene. But below this in smaller writing there is a subtext which says 'The Letter Killeth | The Spirit giveth Life'. Job's mistake is to pray by the letter, not by the spirit. Once more Blake is attacking conventional religion and morality, as he had done ever since *The Marriage of Heaven and Hell*. In the succeeding plates Blake not only shows Job suffering, he also depicts him being visited by God in a whirlwind and experiencing an overwhelming vision of the mysteries of the universe (see fig.55). It is these encounters that give him a new perception of faith and enliven his spirit. In the final scene (fig.56) Job and his family are no longer praying. They are praising the Lord by dancing and singing. They are playing the musical instruments that had formerly

above left
54 *Illustrations of the Book of Job: Plate 1, 'Thus did Job continually'* 1825
Engraving
19.8 × 16.4 (7¾ × 6½)
Tate Gallery

above right
55 *The Book of Job: 'When the Morning Stars Sang Together'* c.1805–10
Watercolour
28 × 18.4 (11 × 7¼)
Pierpont Morgan Library, New York

right
56 *Illustrations of the Book of Job: Plate 21, 'So the Lord blessed the latter end of Job more than the beginning'* 1825
Engraving
19.6 × 14.9 (7¾ × 5⅞)
Tate Gallery

been hanging mute in the tree above their head. It is as though they are at a Gospel revival meeting. In this last plate the church has disappeared, blotted out by the trumpeting of Job's sons.

Blake's version of Job demonstrates his claim that spiritual awareness is a matter of inner vision, not of obeying rules. The story itself – of a man surviving tribulation to achieve deepening awareness – might have been Blake's own.

The Ancients

Unlike Job, Blake and his wife did not have any children. But he might almost have thought that he had, when surrounded by admiring young artists in those last years. Under the leadership of the landscapist Samuel Palmer they formed themselves into a group called The Ancients and referred to Blake's meagre lodgings as the House of the Interpreter. The idea of forming groups or brotherhoods was common in the period. The most celebrated of them was the *Lukasbund* or Brotherhood of St Luke (named after the patron saint of painters) formed by German medieval revivalist painters in Vienna in 1808. The Ancients must certainly have known of the *Lukasbund* (or Nazarenes as they became more familiarly known) in Germany. Like these they affected a medieval style of dress, grew their hair long and wore beards. They had a similar enthusiasm for the Gothic and for northern Renaissance engravers such as Albrecht Dürer and Lucas van Leyden. But whereas the German Nazarenes attempted to revive tradition-al religious painting in the manner of Italian and Northern European painters of the fifteenth and early sixteenth centuries, The Ancients sought to 'medievalise' the landscape. They went to live in the Kent village of Shoreham, where they startled local inhabitants by their odd appearance and behaviour. Blake came to visit them on occasion, but did not join in their make-believe. His outward appearance and manner had always been conventional. Vision for him was an interior matter. His landscapes, too, had been imagined ones; whereas Palmer and his friends sought to find analogues for their spiritual intentions in the actual fields and trees of the Kent countryside. Palmer produced some wonderfully intensified, rich ren-derings. Superficially these might appear to be similar to Blake's *Pastorals* illustrations or some of the backgrounds in *Job*, but at heart their methods are different. So, too, was their politics. Palmer shared neither Blake's radicalism nor his suspicion of organised religion. A High Anglican, he depicted the villagers of Shoreham parading devoutly out of church. He needed role-models, and came to Blake to provide an alternative to the conventional art world of the period. The group desperately needed a master. Soon after Blake's death it began to disperse – though memories of his vision remained with the members throughout their lives.

Dante and the Other World

Even before the *Job* illustrations were complete Blake began work on Linnell's next commission. This was for 100 illustrations to Dante's *Divine Comedy* (see fig. 57). He responded to the project with enthusiasm, even learning some Italian to help him understand Dante more closely. He might also have been stimulated by the thought that his old rival and supporter Flaxman had achieved an international reputation with the *Outlines* to Dante that he had published some thirty years before (see fig. 16). Just as he had taken on Fuseli by illustrating Milton, so now he would confront Flaxman with his own version of Dante. In the years since the publication

57 Dante's 'Divine Comedy': The Inscription over Hell-Gate c. 1824–7 Watercolour 52.7 × 37.4 (20¾ × 14¼) Tate Gallery

HELL Canto 3

HELL Canto 5

58 Dante's 'Divine Comedy': The Circle of the Lustful: Paolo and Francesca c.1824–7 Watercolour 37.2 × 52.2 ($14\frac{5}{8} × 20\frac{1}{2}$) Birmingham Museums and Art Gallery

of Flaxman's designs in 1793, Dante had become increasingly modish. The fantastic side of his visions of Hell, in particular, had appealed to Romantic taste. Although Blake might not have known this, the young French *Romantique* Eugène Delacroix had made a most successful debut depicting Dante and Virgil crossing the Styx into Hell for the Salon in Paris in 1822.[6] He might have heard, however, how the German Nazarenes had recently completed a cycle of frescoes on Italian poets that included a room devoted to Dante in the Casino Massimo in Rome.[7]

Unfinished at the time of his death, the illustrations to Dante show how Blake was at the height of his powers right at the end of his life. Pictures such as *The Circle of the Lustful* (fig.58) or *The Simoniac Pope* (fig.59) combine figures of Michelangelesque vigour and gothic sinuousness with magnificent flickering colour effects. These evoke so vividly a sense of the unearthly regions of Hell, Purgatory and Paradise through which Dante passed in his epic poem, that it might be supposed that Blake was closely following the intentions of the author he was illustrating. But once again he was seeing anew. He had severe reservations about the opinions and visions of the medieval Italian poet. He found it too legalistic and dependent upon the orthodoxy of the Catholic church. He saw what Dante called Hell as in fact being this earth. This can be seen, for example, in their different views on sexual morality. One of the most moving situations that Dante encounters in his journey through Hell is that of Paolo and Francesca. These were two people condemned to Hell because they had committed adultery. Dante has them tell the story of how their love grew,

70

and of Francesca's sufferings at the hands of a tyrannical husband. There seemed every reason to condone their adultery, and Dante is moved by this and by the clear trueness of their love for each other. But despite all extenuating circumstances they have to spend the whole of eternity suffering in Hell because they had broken the rules of the church and sinned. This was clearly a subject that interested Blake strongly and he created one of his finest watercolours illustrating it, as well as working extensively on the engraved version. But for Blake – who condoned free love in theory if not (it would seem) in practice – the case of Paolo and Francesca was to be seen differently. He saw it as being the rules of earth and not of Heaven that had condemned the lovers, and shows them moving triumphantly away from Dante and his blinkered vision. In a striking passage Dante had described how the lovers who were condemned to Hell for their sexual 'incontinence' were to be seen swirling around, buffeted in a whirlwind

> As starlings, ere the winter, in a vast
> innumerable squadron wheel their flight.[8]

Blake takes up this wheeling motif, but instead of showing it as an involuntary motion in which lovers who had allowed their feelings to get the better of them are eternally trapped, he has them form a dynamic spiral which leads them up and out of the picture. It was as though he was providing them with an escape from the endless suffering into which Dante

59 *Dante's 'Divine Comedy': The Simoniac Pope* c.1824–7
Watercolour
52.7 × 36.8
(20¾ × 14½)
Tate Gallery

had plunged them. Blake's criticisms of Dante's account of the other world increased as the Italian poet moved up from Hell through Purgatory to Paradise. For now it seemed to him that the legalistic view of eternity had no way of comprehending the true vision of the Divine. Another image of love is one that brought this out most completely. Dante's magnificent vision is a vision of love as well as religion. For his journey through Hell to Paradise is also a journey to meet again his dead beloved, Beatrice. It is she who guides him through Heaven – a place that Virgil cannot, of course, approach since he is a pagan and therefore condemned to dwell for ever in Hell (another legalistic absurdity Blake took exception to). In Canto 19 of Purgatory, Dante describes Beatrice coming to meet him on an elaborate chariot, drawn by a fantastic gryphon (see fig.60). Dante constructed the gryphon as an allegory of Christ and Beatrice as a symbol of the church. Such thinking ran quite contrary to that of Blake, who saw Dante's vision as being curtailed, rather than enlarged, by his adherence to conventional religion. He saw Dante's 'obedience' as the subjugation of the male imagination to the female will. Yet despite such criticisms he felt the power of Dante's verse and this inspired him to try and match it with visual splendour. The meaning locked up in its obscure iconography has not prevented Blake from investing the image with a wondrous shimmering light, obtained by putting on separate touches of pure colour – a technique not found in watercolour again until Cézanne. Technically, as well as intellectually, Blake was innovating right up to the end.

Blake died 'singing of the things he saw in Heaven' in August 1827, a few months before his seventieth birthday.[9] Despite ill-health, his last years were his most tranquil. For although his worldly success had been limited, he had the satisfaction of knowing that he had remained true to his inner vision throughout the decades of privation and opposition.

60 *Dante's 'Divine Comedy': Beatrice Addressing Dante from the Car* c.1824–7 Watercolour 37.2 × 52.7 ($14\frac{5}{8}$ × $20\frac{3}{4}$) Tate Gallery

EPILOGUE

Blake's Afterlife

While mourned by his immediate associates, Blake's death went all but unnoticed by others. Although occasional references occur to him as a strange, visionary engraver, it was not until the mid-nineteenth century that serious interest in him began to revive. This was not through the offices of Palmer or Linnell – who had both sentimentalised their former visionary approach to landscape – but through that band of Victorian medievalists, the Pre-Raphaelites. Dante Gabriel Rossetti in particular was excited by Blake's imaginative power. As a painter-poet himself, and a deep admirer of Dante, he felt a particular pull towards the earlier visionary's art. It was an associate of Rossetti, Alexander Gilchrist, who produced the first full-length biography of Blake, in 1863. Gilchrist was able to interview many people who had known Blake personally, including Samuel Palmer and George Richmond, and this gives particular interest and authority to his account. Subsequently Blake became a *cause célèbre* for the symbolists, particularly the Irish poet W.B. Yeats. In the early twentieth century he was taken up by the Bloomsbury Group, who celebrated him as a modernist. The leading Bloomsbury art critic Roger Fry even went so far as to call him the only British artist who had a true sense of plastic form. But each generation seems to discover its own Blake. In the 1920s, a more psychological interest in him developed and he became an inspiration to those such as Stanley Spencer and Graham Sutherland who were developing their own individual approaches to artistic spirituality. He was a powerful influence on those who saw Romanticism as a means to create a distinctively British modern style. On the other hand, there was nothing parochial about Blake's impact. He became one of the most admired of British thinkers and poets throughout Europe and North America. Meanwhile a whole industry of Blake studies was growing up. Thanks to the activities of the Blake Trust and other organisations it is possible now to obtain facsimiles of all his major works and both his poems and pictures are readily available in cheap editions. There have been many brilliant works of scholarship expounding his art and his ideas – notably from scholars in North America. Yet despite this, he has not been altogether happily accommodated within broader cultural studies as these have been developed in recent years as a branch of social history.

Aesthetically, too, he still does not quite fit. For those who see art as being primarily about inspiration and individualism he is the paradigm. He exemplifies the stereotypical image of the untameable, genius artist of modern times. Significantly Gulley Jimson, the fictional painter who embodies this assumption absolutely in Joyce Carey's *The Horse's Mouth*, declares that Blake was 'the greatest artist who ever lived' (ch. 1). While Blake represents this new type of artist in one sense, in another he does not. His stance differs markedly from that of artists operating within the élitist avant-garde system of today, even if his example was a contributing factor to its emergence. For this avant-garde has now become the artistic establishment, and uses independence and originality as market ploys. Blake, we must remember, was a genuine outsider in his time. He published himself and put on his own exhibition. From that point of view he has more in common with the myriad semi-professionals of our times who try to keep going by hook or by crook, than he has with those who succeed in their careers through a calculated exploitation of sensation. Blake's individualism relates not to a desire to be different for the sake of difference (or profit), but to a desire to communicate a perception that genuinely came from his particular position. The modern artistic élite may claim Blake as a founding father, but they cannot control his influence. Perhaps it is for this reason that he tends even to this day to inspire deep devotion amongst isolated enthusiasts. The internet is full of messages from those who profess a personal devotion to his art rarely to be found expressed for other artists and writers. What is clear is that his thought, verse and images still communicate a challenging and exciting perception to those who are prepared to look and listen.

Appendix: Extracts from Blake's Writings

All these texts have been taken from David Erdman's anthology of Blake's writings but can also be found in an anthology edited by Sir Geoffrey Keynes (see Bibliography).

From 'Auguries of Innocence' (c.1800–5)

> To see a World in a Grain of Sand
> And a Heaven in a Wild Flower
> Hold Infinity in the palm of your hand
> And Eternity in an hour.
>
> ...
>
> God Appears and God is Light
> To those poor Souls who dwell in Night.
> But does a Human Form Display
> To those who Dwell in Realms of Day.
>
> [Erdman (ed.), p.490]

Songs of Experience

'The Sick Rose' (1794)

> O Rose, thou art sick!
> The invisible worm
> That flies in the night,
> in the howling storm:
>
> Has found out thy bed
> Of crimson joy:
> And his dark secret love
> Does thy life destroy.
>
> [Erdman (ed.), p.23]

'The Tyger' (1794)

> Tyger Tyger, burning bright
> In the forests of the night;
> What immortal hand or eye,
> Could frame thy fearful symmetry?
>
> In what distant deeps or skies
> Burnt the fire of thine eyes?
> On what wings dare he aspire?
> What the hand dare sieze the fire?
>
> And what shoulder, & what art,
> Could twist the sinews of thy heart?
> And when thy heart began to beat,
> What dread hand? & what dread feet?

> What the hammer? what the chain,
> In what furnace was thy brain?
> what the anvil? what dread grasp
> Dare its deadly terrors clasp?
>
> When the stars threw down their spears,
> And water'd heaven with their tears:
> Did he smile his work to see?
> Did he who made the Lamb make thee?
>
> Tyger Tyger, burning bright
> In the forests of the night:
> What immortal hand or eye
> Dare frame thy fearful symmetry?
>
> [Erdman (ed.), pp.24–5]

The Marriage of Heaven and Hell

From *Proverbs of Hell* (1790–3)

> A fool sees not the same tree that a wise man sees. (pl.5, p.35)
>
> Eternity is in love with the productions of time. (pl.7, p.36)
>
> Prisons are built with stones of Law, Brothels with bricks of Religion. (pl.8, p.36)
>
> The nakedness of woman is the work of God. (pl.8, p.36)
>
> As the caterpillar chooses the fairest leaves to lay her eggs on, so the priest lays his curse on the fairest joys. (pl.9, p.37)
>
> Opposition is true Friendship. (pl.20, p.42)
>
> One Law for the Lion & Ox is Oppression. (pl.24, p.44)
>
> [Erdman (ed.), pp.35–44]

From *Milton* (1804)

> And did those feet in ancient time
> walk upon England's mountains green;
> And was the holy Lamb of God
> On England's pleasant pastures seen!
>
> And did the Countenance Divine
> Shine forth upon our clouded hills?
> And was Jerusalem builded here
> Among these dark Satanic Mills?

Bring me my Bow of burning gold:
Bring me my Arrows of desire:
Bring me my Spear: O clouds unfold!
Bring me my Chariot of fire.

I will not cease from Mental Fight,
Nor shall my Sword sleep in my hand:
Till we have built Jerusalem,
In Englands green & pleasant Land.

[Erdman (ed.), pl.2, p.96]

'I rose up at the dawn of day' (n.d.)

I am in God's presence night & day,
And he never turns his face away.

[Erdman (ed.), p.481]

'Eternity' (n.d.)

He who binds to himself a joy
Does the winged life destroy.
But he who kisses the joy as it flies
Lives in eternity's sun rise.

[Erdman (ed.), p.470]

From *Jerusalem* (1804–18)

I must Create a System or be enslav'd by
another Man's.
I will not Reason & Compare: my business is to
Create.

[Erdman (ed.), pl.10, p.153]

From 'Annotations to Reynolds's Discourses'
(*c.*1798–1809)

To Generalize is to be an Idiot. To Particularize is
the Alone Distinction of Merit. (p.641)

... the Bad Artist seems to Copy a Great Deal.
The Good one Really Does Copy a Great Deal.
(p.645)

Every Eye Sees differently. (p.648)

Reynolds Thinks that Man Learns all that he
knows. I say on the Contrary that Man Brings
All that he has or Can have Into the World
with him. Man is born like a Garden ready
Planted & Sown. This World is too poor to
produce one Seed. (p.656)

If Art was Progressive We should have had
Mich. Angelos & Rafaels to Succeed & to
Improve upon each other. But it is not so.
Genius dies with its Possessor & comes not
again till Another is Born with It. (p.656)

[Erdman (ed.), pp.641–56]

From *A Descriptive Catalogue* (1809)

A Spirit and a Vision are not, as the modern
philosophy supposes, a cloudy vapour, or a
nothing: they are organized and minutely
articulated beyond all that the mortal and
perishing nature can produce.

Painting ... exults and exists in immortal
thoughts.

The great and golden rule of art, as well as of
life, is this: That the more distinct, sharp, and
wirey the bounding line, the more perfect the
work of art ...

[Erdman (ed.), p.526]

The Ghost of Abel (1822)

From address 'To LORD BYRON in the
Wilderness'

... Nature has no Outline:
but Imagination has. Nature has no Tune: but
Imagination has!
Nature has no Supernatural & dissolves:
Imagination is Eternity.

[Erdman (ed.), p.270]

From 'Marginalia to Berkeley's Siris' (n.d.)

Man is All Imagination God is Man & exists in us
& we in him.

[Erdman (ed.), p.664]

From *Laocoon*

You must leave Fathers & Mothers & Houses &
Lands if they stand in the way of ART.

Jesus & his Apostles & Disciples were all Artists.

Where any view of Money exists, Art cannot be
carried on.

Art can never exist without Naked Beauty dis
played.

[Erdman (ed.), pp.273–5]

From *On Virgil* (*c.*1820)

Rome and Greece swept Art into their Maw &
destroy'd it ...
Grecian is Mathematic Form:
Gothic is Living Form.

[Erdman (ed.), p.270]

Notes

Introduction

1 *Jerusalem*, pl. 3, in *The Complete Poetry and Prose of William Blake*, ed. David V. Erdman, Berkeley and Los Angeles 1982, p.145.

2 *On Virgil*, in Erdman (ed.), p.153.

3 *Jerusalem*, pl. 10. The speaker is Los.

4 *Milton*, in Erdman (ed.), p.96.

5 *Marriage of Heaven and Hell*, in Erdman (ed.), p.36.

Chapter 1

1 Peter Ackroyd, *Blake*, London 1995, p.35.

2 Erdman (ed.), p.664.

3 Erdman (ed.), p.656.

4 *On Virgil*, in Erdman (ed.), p.270.

5 Benjamin West, *The Death of Wolfe*, 1770, oil on canvas, 151 × 213.4 cm, Ottawa, National Gallery of Canada.

6 B. Nicolson, *John Hamilton Mortimer*, exh. cat., Iveagh Bequest, Kenwood 1968, p.31.

7 Martin Butlin, *The Paintings and Drawings of William Blake*, London 1981, p.32.

Chapter 2

1 *The Marriage of Heaven and Hell*, in Erdman (ed.), p.36.

2 In a letter to Mrs Flaxman, in Erdman (ed.), p.708.

3 Erdman (ed.), p.197.

4 Roy Porter, *A Social History of Madness*, London 1989, p.64.

5 Daniel 4: 33.

6 *Macbeth*, I. vii.

7 Erdman (ed.), p.507.

8 P. Tomory, *The Life and Art of Henry Fuseli*, London 1972, p.119.

Chapter 3

1 Erdman (ed.), p.637.

2 Peter Ackroyd, *Blake*, London 1995, p.203.

3 *Milton*, pl.9, l.5.

4 23 September 1800; Erdman (ed.), p.711.

5 Erdman (ed.), p.635.

6 Anne-Louis Girodet-Trioson, *The Ghosts of French Heroes ... received by the Ghosts of Ossian and his Valiant Warriors*, exhibited 1802, Musée National du Château, Rueil-Malmaison.

Chapter 4

1 Sharon Turner, *History of the Anglo-Saxon*, 4 vols., London 1799–1805

2 L. Colley, *Britons: Forging the Nation 1707–1837*, London and Newhaven 1992, p.18.

3 *Jerusalem*, pl.92.

4 *Milton*, pl.23, l.47.

5 *Marriage of Heaven and Hell*, pl.7.

6 E. Delacroix, *Dante and Virgil in Hell*, 1822, Louvre, Paris.

7 These are by Joseph Anton Koch. See Keith Andrews, *The Nazarenes*, Oxford 1964, pp.69–72.

8 Canto V, ll.40–1, in *Dante Translated into English Verse*, ed. I.C. Wright, London 1854, p.20.

9 As described by George Richmond in a letter to Samuel Palmer, *The Letters of William Blake*, ed. Geoffrey Keynes, Oxford 1980, p.171.

Photographic Credits

Chronology

1757 Born on 28 November at 28 Broad Street, Golden Square, London, the son of James Blake, a hosier.

1767 Enters Henry Pars's drawing school, 101 Strand.

1772 Apprenticed on 4 August to the engraver James Basire, at 31 Great Queen Street, for a period of seven years. Amongst other projects Blake is set to make copies of the royal tombs in Westminster Abbey.

1779 On 8 October enters the Royal Academy schools to study engraving. Meets the sculptor John Flaxman, a fellow student who was to become an important friend and benefactor.

1780 Exhibits a watercolour, *Death of Earl Goodwin*, at the Royal Academy. He subsequently exhibits at the Academy in 1784, 1785, 1799, 1800 and 1809.

1782 On 18 August marries Catherine Boucher (or Butcher), the daughter of a market gardener. The couple set up house in 23 Green Street, Leicester Fields.

1783 First book of poems, *Poetical Sketches*, printed.

1784 Father dies on 4 July. In the autumn Blake moves back to the street of his birth, 27 Broad Street, and sets up a partnership with his former fellow student James Parker. At some point over the next three years the partnership is dissolved.

1785 Moves to 28 Poland Street. Possibly his partnership with James Parker is dissolved at this time.

1787 Robert, his favourite brother, whom he had involved in his projects, dies. He is buried in Bunhill Fields in February.

1788 Produces his first works using his special method of illuminated printing. These are *There is No Natural Religion* and *All Religions are One*.

1789 Publishes first major independent works, *Songs of Innocence* and *The Book of Thel*.

1790 Moves in the autumn to 13 Hercules Buildings, Lambeth.

1791 The first part of his intended poem *The French Revolution* is typeset for the radical publisher Joseph Johnson. In view of the political situation, however, this project is not proceeded with.

1792 Mother Catherine dies and is buried in Bunhill Fields.

1793 Publishes *The Marriage of Heaven and Hell* (begun 1790), *Visions of the Daughters of Albion*, *America* and *For Children: The Gates of Paradise*.

1794 Publishes *Songs of Innocence and Experience*, *Europe* and *The First Book of Urizen*.

1795 Publishes *The Song of Los*, *The Book of Ahania*, *The Book of Los*.

1796 Illustrates Edward Young's *Night Thoughts*, begins work on *The Book of Vala* and *The Four Zoas*.

1797 Commissioned by Flaxman to illustrate Thomas Gray's *Poems*.

1799 First documented work for Thomas Butts, the patron who is to become central for Blake's survival as an artist over the next twenty years.

1800 On 18 September moves to Felpham, near Chichester, under the patronage of the poet William Hayley.

1803 Returns with his wife to London in September, settling in 17 South Molton Street.

1804 Tried for sedition in January on a charge brought against him by the trooper Scolfield at Chichester. Acquitted.

1803–10 Working on *Milton, a Poem*.

1804–20 Working on last great poem, *Jerusalem, the Emanation of the Giant Albion*.

1808 Illustrations to Robert Blair's *The Grave* are published by R.H. Cromek. They are engraved by Luigi Schiavonetti.

1809 In May holds an exhibition of his work at the house of his brother James, 28 Broad Street. Although scheduled to close in September, this exhibition lasts well into the following year. Publishes a *Descriptive Catalogue* to accompany this.

1812 Exhibits three temperas and a watercolour at the *Associated Painters in Watercolours*.

1818 Meets John Linnell in June, who was henceforth to become his most important patron and supporter. Through Linnell Blake met the watercolourist and astrologer John Varley, as well as the artists Samuel Palmer, George Richmond and Edward Calvert who later formed The Ancients group.

1819 Draws 'Visionary Heads' for John Varley.

1821 Moves to 3 Fountain Court, the Strand. Dr Thornton's *Pastorals of Virgil* is published, containing wood-engravings by Blake. Forced to sell his collection of prints, to Colnaghi.

1823 Linnell commissions Blake to engrave his illustrations to the Book of Job.

1824 Linnell commissions Blake to make illustrations to Dante, and to produce engravings after them. By the time of his death he will have produced 102 drawings of varying degrees of completeness and 7 engravings.

1826 In March engravings of *Illustrations of the Book of Job* are published.

1827 Dies on 12 August at 3 Fountain Court.

1831 Catherine Blake dies on 18 October.

1863 Alexander Gilchrist's *The Life of William Blake* is published.

bliography

Works by Blake

e most accurate edition of the
mplete writings of Blake is
vid V. Erdman (ed.),
*e Complete Poetry and Prose of
illiam Blake*, Berkeley and Los
ngeles 1982 (1st pub. 1965).
1 older version still much used is
offrey Keynes (ed.),
*e Complete Writings of William
ake*, Oxford 1966 (1st pub.
57). For the illuminated books
David V. Erdman,
Illuminated Blake, London
75, and David Bindman,
*Complete Graphic Works of
illiam Blake*, London 1978.

ere are several facsimile editions
ndividual illuminated books by
ke. The William Blake Trust has
duced a six-volume series in
sociation with the Tate Gallery.
e most important Œuvre
italogue covering Blake's
intings and drawings is Martin
itlin, *The Paintings and Drawings
William Blake*, 2 vols., London
81.

ake's commercial designs and
ok illustrations can be found in
bert N. Essick, *William Blake's
mmercial Book Illustrations*,
ford 1991; Robert Blair,
e Grave, facsimile introduced by
bert N. Essick and Morton D.
iley, London 1982; *William
ake's Designs for Edward Young's
ght Thoughts*, ed. David V.
dman, John E. Grant, Edward J.
se and Michael J. Tolley, 2 vols.,
ford 1980; Irene Tayler, *Blake's
ustrations to the Poems of Gray*,
ndon 1971.

Studies on Blake

ckroyd, Peter, *Blake*, London
95.
ndman, David, *Blake as an Artist*,
ford 1977.
unt, Anthony, *The Art of William
ake*, New York 1959.
mon, S. Foster, *A Blake
ctionary: Ideas and Symbols of
illiam Blake*, London 1973.

Erdman, David V., *Blake: Prophet
against Empire*, Princeton 1954.

Essick, Robert N., *William Blake,
Printmaker*, Princeton 1980.

Frye, Northrop, *Fearful Symmetry*,
Princeton 1969
(1st pub. 1947).

Gilchrist, Alexander, *The Life of
William Blake*, London 1863.

Paley, Morton D., *William Blake*,
London 1978.

Glossary: Blake's Mythology

The following is a brief note of
Blake's principal characters as
developed largely in his prophetic
books. Blake never gives a
definition of his characters, and
their meaning is extrapolated from
the roles they play in his writing.
The best guide to them is S. Foster
Damon's *A Blake Dictionary* (see
Bibliography).

Albion A common poetical name
for England, used by Blake to
personify the country.

Emanation Is the female counterpart of the essentially bisexual
male. **Jerusalem**, for example, is the
emanation of **Albion**.

Enitharmon Is spiritual beauty,
the **emanation** of **Los**.

Jerusalem Stands for Liberty. She
is the **emanation** of **Albion** and a
spiritual inspiration for all
mankind.

Los Personifies poetry, the creative
imagination.

Luvah Represents love and sexual
energy.

Oothoon Represents thwarted
love. The third daughter of **Los** and
Enitharmon she is also the 'soft soul
of America'.

Orc Is the spirit of Revolution, the
firstborn of **Los** and **Enitharmon**.

Urizen Stands for Reason. In
Blake's eyes he is the limiter of
energy, the vengeful lawmaker.

Vala Is the goddess of nature.

Index